HOPE
THROUGH THE
TRUTH

Standing in the Gap in America

STANLEY HOLSTEIN

Hope Through the Truth—Standing in the Gap in America.

Copyright © 2021 Stanley Holstein.

All rights reserved. No portion of this book may be reproduced, stored in a retrieval system, or transmitted in any form or by any means—electronic, mechanical, photocopy, recording, scanning, or other—except for brief quotations in critical reviews or articles, without the prior written permission of the publisher.

Published by SLH Publishing; P.O. Box 177, Bluffton, OH 45817
website: https://hopethroughthetruth.com

All Scripture quotations, unless otherwise indicated, are taken from the Holy Bible, New International Version®, NIV®. Copyright ©1973, 1978, 1984, 2011 by Biblica, Inc.® Used by permission of Zondervan. All rights reserved worldwide. www.zondervan.com The "NIV" and "New International Version" are trademarks registered in the United States Patent and Trademark Office by Biblica, Inc.®

Quotations taken from *Crazy Love,* copyright © 2008 by Francis Chan, are used by permission of David C. Cook and may not be further reproduced. All rights reserved.

Quotations taken from *My Utmost for His Highest* by Oswald Chambers, copyright © 1935 by Dodd Mead & Co., renewed © 1963 by the Oswald Chambers Publications Assn., Ltd., are used by permission of Discovery House Publishers, Box 3566, Grand Rapids, MI 49501. All rights reserved.

Quotations taken from *True North: Discovering God's Way in a Changing World,* copyright © 2002 by Gary Inrig are used by permission of Our Daily Bread Publishing, Box 3566, Grand Rapids, MI 49501. All rights reserved.

Quotations taken from *The Gathering Storm—Secularism, Culture, and the Church*, by R. Albert Mohler Jr., copyright © 2020 by R. Albert Mohler Jr., are used by permission of Thomas Nelson. www.thomasnelson.com.

Quotations taken from *The Purpose-Driven Life* by Richard Warren, copyright © 2002 by Richard Warren, are used by permission of Zondervan. www.zondervan.com.

Quotations taken from *Roaring Lambs: A Gentle Plan to Radically Change Your World* by Bob Briner, copyright © 1993 by Bob Briner, are used by permission of Zondervan. www.zondervan.com.

Quotations taken from:

Free to Believe: The Battle over Religious Liberty in America by Luke Goodrich, copyright © 2019 by Luke W. Goodrich;

Radical—Taking Back Your Faith from the American Dream by David Platt, copyright © 2010 by David Platt; and

Tender Warrior, by Stu Weber, copyright © 1993 by Stu Weber, are used by permission of Penguin Random House, www.penguinrandomhouse.com.

Quotations taken from the *Holman Bible Dictionary* Copyright © 1991 by Holman Bible Publishers are reprinted and used by permission of Holman Bible Publishers. All rights reserved. International copyright secured.

"Prison Fellowship" and "Prison Fellowship Ministries" are trademarks of Prison Fellowship Ministries.

Any websites, phone numbers, or company or product information printed in this book are offered as a resource and are not intended in any way to be or to imply an endorsement by the publisher, nor does the publisher vouch for the existence, content, or services of these sites, phone numbers, companies, or products.

ISBN 978-1-7360865-1-3 (eBook)
ISBN 978-1-7360865-0-6 (paperback)
ISBN 978-1-7360865-2-0 (hard cover)

Printed in the United States of America.

Special thanks to the following contributors:

Cover Design by 100Covers.com
Interior Design by FormattedBooks.com
Editing by Kevin Miller, www.kevinmillerxi.com

To the three most influential people in my life:

Mom and Dad, the first kingdom of heaven ambassadors I ever knew.
Mom, a selfless woman who showed compassion and love
while helping me believe I could do anything if I tried.
Dad, who showed me I could live for the Lord unafraid.
Susie, my best friend and wife, who served as the lone
Christian in our household for eleven years and has walked
side by side with me for more than four decades.

Table of Contents

Introduction ix

Chapter 1: A Blessed Life 1
Chapter 2: Our Purpose 9
Chapter 3: The Calling 17
Chapter 4: Our Role in God's Plan 29
Chapter 5: The Struggle Against Self 33
Chapter 6: The Struggle with the Word of God 43
Chapter 7: The Struggle with Servanthood 55
Chapter 8: The Struggle Against Flesh and Blood 73
Chapter 9: The Struggle Against Spiritual Forces 85
Chapter 10: Persecuting Messengers of The Truth 103
Chapter 11: The State of the Union 115
Chapter 12: The Opportunity is Today 119
Chapter 13: Retirement—A Golden Opportunity 141
Chapter 14: Your Assigned Area of Operation 151

Conclusion 173
Notes 181

Introduction

Is something significant missing from my spiritual life?

I don't recall giving much consideration to this question as a teenager or young adult. My attention was focused on the task or activity at hand. In retrospect, I now realize I spent a considerable amount of time searching for one thing or another through the years. As a teenager I went camping often. Before each trip, I would check my backpack to ensure I had all the necessities for my outing. Later, as a young man, I worked for a house builder. At the end of each workday, we would search the area to locate the tools that had been strewn about the jobsite. This pattern continued throughout my career. As a businessman, I would often travel for five days at a time. I would double check my luggage to ensure I had packed all the necessary clothing and work materials required for the trip. In each of these instances and many others, whether at work or play, I was searching, not so much for what I had gathered but for any necessary thing that might be missing. I didn't consider myself prepared for the task at hand until I determined nothing important was missing.

If such a question and concept is so important to my physical life, it seems it would also be important to my spiritual life. Whether we consider ourselves "religious" or not, we all have a soul, a spiritual aspect to our being. An entire library of books, articles, and videos has been produced on this topic, addressed to people of every spiritual persuasion. I have read a quote, credited to different persons, that says, "The two greatest days in your life are the day you were born and the day you discover the reason you were born."

So, is something significant missing from my spiritual life? This is a valid question for me at any time because I can always improve. Depending on when I answer this question, the response will vary. In some days or seasons, more is missing. At other times, less is missing. On rare, brief occasions I may conclude that nothing is missing. This question is directed at me! Since I believe the Holy Bible is the one flawless, eternal truth, I must admit at the outset that examining this issue is a scary proposition given my sinful nature. Scripture tells me God observes, examines, and tests me. It also instructs me to examine and test myself by regularly looking in the mirror, God's Word, to determine if I am walking according to my faith. Through this process the Holy Spirit will highlight those areas of my spiritual life that need improvement. The beauty is, I will be the only human involved in this process. God won't be waiting to scold, accuse, or condemn me for my shortcomings either. He wants me to improve and succeed. So, after my self-assessment, the ensuing conversation will only be between God and me. No one else! It's personal!

Is it time for you to take a long look in the mirror? Is now a good time to ask yourself if anything significant is missing from your spiritual life? Some may say, "I don't believe in God as Creator or the Bible as truth." That is certainly your prerogative. Each person determines what they accept as truth. Others may say, "I do believe in God and the Bible. I am operating squarely within God's will." If this is true of your life, may God continue to bless you mightily in your service to the kingdom of heaven. Most folks I know fall somewhere in between these two examples. Either they have not yet accepted Jesus Christ as Lord and Savior, or they have but are still trying to determine God's plan for their lives. Back to the initial question once again. For me and many others, the answer is "Yes" or "I'm not sure." Either of these answers presents us with no less than three additional questions.

- What significant thing is missing from my spiritual life?
- What is my specific purpose in life?
- What is truth?

The answers to these questions have eternal implications. In the following pages, I provide answers from God's Word as I understand it. My attempt to write has already proven profitable for me. It has served as an extended journaling exercise, producing some eye-opening realizations. I have considered and tried to answer honestly, for myself, every question posed in these pages. Some of my responses were far from flattering. Yet, I believe God will bless me if I am bold enough to make the necessary effort to correct the shortcomings he has shown me. So far, this has been a convicting, cathartic, and mobilizing trek. Still, it is far from over. Will you join me? I hope so. Difficult journeys don't produce quite as much anxiety if you have company along the way. I'm convinced the venture will be profitable for each of us, if we dare. Should you decide to make this trek, God won't be waiting to scold, accuse, or condemn you for your shortcomings either. He wants you to improve and succeed. So, after your self-assessment, the ensuing conversation will only be between you and God. No one else! It's personal!

Chapter 1

A Blessed Life

> How beautiful on the mountains are the feet of those who bring good news, who proclaim peace, who bring good tidings, who proclaim salvation, who say to Zion, "Your God reigns!" (Isaiah 52:7)

Jesus Christ is my Lord and Savior. The Holy Bible is God's "owner's manual" for me. God's Word tells me everything I need to know about living here on earth. It tells me the reason I was born, my purpose for being, how I should live, why I should live in his prescribed manner, and where I will spend eternity. Some may ask, "How did you get to this place in your life? By what path or process did you arrive at these decisions?" Both are good questions. Let's start at the beginning.

A Firm Foundation

God has blessed me mightily throughout my life. I was born the second of four children in the hills of West Virginia to parents who were both Christians. At the time of my birth, Dad was a full-time telephone lineman and a full-time Baptist preacher as well. Mom was a devoted homemaker. Dad served twice as the pastor of small churches. He wasn't an educated man, but he studied the Word of God diligently. As a result, the Holy Spirit rewarded Dad with a solid understanding of Scripture and the ability to bring God's Word to life with power.

Dad had two passions, evangelism and singing. He would travel to small towns in West Virginia to preach. Most of these towns had a church building that they used for church services but no pastor. He also took vacations from work to preach at revivals. Sometimes he would take me with him. If a visiting minister or missionary came into town, a welcome bed was waiting at our house. Prayer and Bible study were integral parts of our home life. Dad also sang in a Christian quartet. Anne, my sister, played piano and sang with another Christian group. You might say I was born into the church. If the church doors were open, our family was there. So, my earliest memories were of a loving family devoted to the Lord, each other, and the body of believers.

Mom and Dad were content with their lot in life. They had peace and joy. They didn't complain, at least not to us children, about the worries of the world. As a child, I didn't necessarily connect their contentment and joy with their faith in God, but there was one thing I did learn early in life about my parents' relationship with the Lord. It came from conversations they had between themselves or with fellow believers that weren't directed to me. They loved God and his Son, Jesus. Mom and Dad talked about and acted as if God and Jesus Christ were real. It seemed my parents knew them personally because they did. Early in life I learned that God was real, he loved me, and Jesus died for my sins.

Another powerful impact they had on me at an early age was how their love of God translated into love for others. They treated the crippled and the poor with friendship and dignity, giving help as they were able. Folks who came to our house in need never left with money, but they always left with food or clothing. If they happened to stop by at mealtime, they were invited to eat with us. Mom and Dad understood the powerful witness of engaging others with acceptance and respect. Every person they met was a believer who needed encouragement or a lost soul who needed to see the love of God.

When I was very young, one particular man would come to our house with some regularity. Sometimes we would come home, and he would be sitting outside the house waiting for us. Once we got inside, Mom would ask, "Would you like me to run you some bath water?" He would always accept. He would bathe, eat, visit for a while, and then leave. Dad would offer to give this man a ride wherever he was going. I don't recall him ever accepting the offer. Mom and Dad took God's two greatest commandments seriously, to love God and to love other people. They didn't just tell me about God's love. Most importantly, they showed me his love. They desired their children to choose to love God too. Such a foundation was priceless to me, making an eternal impact.

Some other relatives and a number of family friends had seemingly mastered loving others. One in particular was Uncle Arthur, known to us as Ott. His words, actions, and demeanor exuded love, peace, and acceptance. I can never remember Ott speaking negatively about another person. Nor did I ever see a child who wouldn't go to him the first time they met him. I am certain almost everyone who spent time with Ott felt his love for and acceptance of them. They felt his genuine desire to be in their presence and viewed themselves as more valued than they did before they met him. We all want and need that.

My friend, Jeff, told me about his childhood memory of Arlie, a mature Christian, who was approaching seventy years of age. Jeff remembered Arlie as a quiet, gentle, peaceful Christian who never said or did anything wrong. One day, Jeff overheard someone asking where they could find Arlie. The reply was "Oh, he's probably out back humming himself to death." Arlie's joy in the Lord exuded from his very being without him having to say a word. He made a tremendous impression on a young man through his consistent demeanor of love.

The peace and joy exhibited by Ott, Arlie, and others like them made them different from most people. True peace and joy only come from one source: God's indwelling Holy Spirit. It cannot be mimicked by those who don't have the Holy Spirit. Many people may exhibit earthly happiness and contentment, but these are temporary conditions at best. People who truly love the Lord possess something significantly distinct from most other humans even if we are unsure of what the "something" is. When they speak or show God's love to us, we tend to listen.

Two Mysteries of Grace

I am so thankful I was born into a Christian household. However, I had my own bull-headed ideas about life as I grew up. I was not attempting to live for the Lord when I left Mom and Dad's home to establish my own. Yet, God continued to reinforce the foundational teachings of faith I had learned as a boy from Mom, Dad, and others. He accomplished this through what I now call the "two mysteries of grace," which I will explain shortly.

God has revealed mysteries to those who believe in him. These include the gospel message, Jesus Christ, and Christ living in those who believe. The unsaved do not comprehend these things. The New Testament speaks of several fundamental, life-changing mysteries involving God's will regarding the redemption of humanity, Jesus's role in redemption, and those who may receive God's grace.

- "He [God] made known to us the mystery of his will according to his good pleasure, which he purposed in Christ, to be put into effect when the times reach their fulfillment—to bring unity to all things in heaven and on earth under Christ" (Ephesians 1:9–10).
- "In reading this, then, you will be able to understand my insight into the mystery of Christ, which was not made known to people in other generations as it has now been revealed by the Spirit to God's holy apostles and prophets. This mystery is that through the gospel the Gentiles are heirs together with Israel, members together of one body, and sharers together in the promise in Christ Jesus" (Ephesians 3:4–6).

Jesus Christ, during his brief walk on this earth according to God's plan:

- Provided a pathway for all humanity to be reconciled (restored to right relationship) to God rather than being condemned to everlasting destruction for breaking his law;
- Extended the offer of redemption to every person, not just the Jews; and
- Prepared a small group of humans to proclaim the gospel message to the world after Jesus ascended into heaven.

Only a comparatively few people, most of whom were living in and around the Middle East in the first century, understood the significance of Jesus's death or the message of his ragtag group of followers known as Christians. For most of the first-century world, Jesus Christ remained a mystery. Twenty centuries later, I have my own mysteries about God and Jesus to unravel. For twenty-six years I have been blessed to have the privilege of walking with Jesus Christ as my Lord and Savior. As I have journeyed with the Lord, God has faithfully placed believers in my life to help me along the way. After all these years, I accept God's plan for my life, even the parts I don't fully understand.

Two of those things that I appreciate most I call the "two mysteries of grace." They amaze me as much today as the day I committed my life to Jesus Christ.

First, God knew before the beginning of the world every decision I would make, every sin I would commit, and the price he would have to pay to bring me into a right relationship with him. Yet, God still sent his one and only Son, Jesus Christ, to earth to die for me. I don't quite get it. The Creator died for an ungrateful creation, me, so I might have life eternal with him. If I were God, having all power and control, I would have devised a plan of redemption that didn't require my Son to die. (This is just one of a million differences between God and me.)

God designed his plan to meet every requirement of his perfect holiness and justice under his law to redeem me (pay the debt for my sins) while at the same time proving to me how much he loves me. So, God paid the greatest possible price for my redemption through the sacrifice of Jesus Christ. I understand Jesus gave his life for everyone's sins, but I'm only talking about my sins right now. Some two thousand years ago, Jesus Christ left his Father's side in heaven, wrapped himself in skin and bone, walked this earth, lived a sinless life, and then allowed himself to be tortured, crucified, and separated from his Father while dying on a cross in my place for my sins. If I were the only person who ever chose to live for the Lord, Jesus would still have come to earth. He did all that for me. It's personal!

Second, God gave me life, knowing I would choose to reject Jesus for decades. After giving me life, God could have allowed me to die while I was lost in my sins, which is exactly what I deserved. In fact, there were at least a couple of times when I came close to dying, and should have died, while lost. Instead, God protected me in my rebellion while placing one Christian after another in my sinful path to befriend me and point me toward Jesus. The Holy Spirit convicted me, and I finally gave my life to Christ. As if he hadn't done enough already, God continued to pour more Christians into my life after I was saved. Once again, God chose to prove to me that he doesn't want me or anyone else to be separated from him eternally. So, he chose me and pursued me while utilizing an enormous amount of precious human resources in the process. It's personal!

Some may say this shouldn't be a mystery since Scripture explains to us, in different ways and through numerous passages, exactly what God did and why he did it. Yet, I continue to struggle to comprehend it completely. I would like to be able to say I understand God's lavish, perfect love for me, but I don't—not really. My human mind doesn't have the capacity to truly understand agape (God's pure) love. What kind of God is willing to die for his own creation who rejected him? Great question! A God who is loving beyond description, among other things. One thing I can state with certainty is I am eternally grateful to God, who called me and placed his Holy Spirit within me, and to Jesus, who gave his life for me.

I like the way Francis Chan describes his relationship with God. Regarding the origin of the title for his book, *Crazy Love,* Francis says, "The idea of *Crazy Love* has to do with our relationship with God . . . It's probably the most insane statement you could make to say that the eternal Creator of this universe is in love with me. There is a response that ought to take place in believers, a crazy reaction to that love."[1] I find it very encouraging to know other people who love the Lord, know his Word, and are willing to admit they also struggle with the sheer enormity of God's grace.

- Randy Allen, senior minister at Bethel Church of Christ in Ada, Ohio, while preaching a series on Hosea, described God's grace as "scandalous, outrageous, and relentless" as God pursued an undeserving people.
- Francis Chan explains his struggle humbly and simply in *Crazy Love*, saying, "Heavenly Father, thank You for Your grace. Your forgiveness is SO good that I struggle with believing it at times. Thank You for rescuing me from myself and giving me Your Holy Spirit. Your love is better than life."[2]

I have accepted these "two mysteries of grace" as I call them, God's grace and his continual pursuit of me using all available resources, even though I don't fully understand either. While thinking about the many Christians that God chose to place in my path and those who were most influential in my decision to accept Jesus Christ as Lord and Savior, I came to the following conclusions.

- Many of these people were a generation or more older than me.
- All these people desired an intimate relationship with me.
- All these people cared about my well-being here on earth and eternally.

In hindsight it is clear to me that God was utilizing Christians to guide me in my adult life as he had used Mom and Dad to guide me in my formative years. He was also giving me examples of the future role he desired me to adopt to serve him in the lives of others after my conversion.

Chapter 2

Our Purpose

> So, whether you eat or drink or whatever you do, do it all for the glory of God. (1 Corinthians 10:31)

Before I can reasonably determine whether or not something significant is missing from my spiritual life, I need to understand my purpose for existing. Why am I here? What is my purpose on earth? These are questions we've all heard, pondered, and possibly discussed with others at some point. The answers are important to each of us since they impact how we view our contribution to society, our personal accomplishments in life, and dictate most, if not all, of the actions we take. The responses are as varied as the people who make up our world. Philosophers, psychologists, scientists, religious leaders, and many others have produced videos and films and written books or articles detailing their responses to these questions. Self-help gurus and motivational speakers travel the country, holding seminars and selling their books and videos while proposing their pathway to happiness, enlightenment, and achievement.

Searching for My Purpose

With the guidance of Mom, Dad, and others, I thought I found my purpose in God's Word. So, when I was twelve years old, I committed my life to Jesus Christ and was baptized into him. Unfortunately, my life didn't seem to change much after my baptism. Instead of developing a closer relationship with the

Lord, I felt like I was drifting further away from him. It didn't take long for my rebellious nature to take over. I refused to recognize the value of my earliest teachings and turned away from the Lord. As a teenager I stopped going to church altogether. An explanation is in order here. My dear friend, Rick, who happens to be a minister, goes bonkers every time he hears a believer refer to a building as "the church." His emphatic response to such a statement is, "You don't go to church; you are the church." Rick is correct, and I love him, but I hope you understand what I'm saying. It was nearly two decades before I started attending church services again. As a young teenager, I couldn't wait to be sixteen, so I could drive a car. It seemed like the year between my fifteenth and sixteenth birthdays took an eternity to pass. Once I could drive, I couldn't wait to turn twenty-one, so I would be "legal" in every respect. When I graduated from high school, I also graduated to a greater variety of sins. No matter what I tried, the gratification was short-lived.

Looking back over the decades, I realize how much precious time I wasted living without Christ. I can also see three other devastating results of my sins: guilt, shame, and pride. The guilt and shame came from my willful, repetitive sin because I knew what I was doing was wrong. Satan helped intensify these emotions by telling me I was buried so deep in sin that I could never be forgiven. Thankfully, I didn't accept the lie completely because of what I had been taught about God's grace. Nevertheless, the lie did help me decide, erroneously and pridefully, that I could turn my life around on my own. In my mind, I needed to turn my life around before returning to the Lord. The guilt and shame were obvious results of my sin. It was my pride, combined with the guilt and shame, that made the combination almost lethal for me.

Thanks be to God Almighty, he loved me even as I rebelled. Because of his love for me, he had a plan for my life and he put it into action. Fortunately for me, "Many are the plans in a man's heart, but it is the Lord's purpose that prevails" (Proverbs 19:21). I couldn't see it as it was happening. In retrospect, I can see clearly. God was patiently and persistently insinuating his plan into my life. This became a repetitive theme in my life, ultimately saving me. God had no intention of abandoning me, even though I was trying my best to abandon him.

I attended West Virginia University for my first year at college. I wasn't there to study or learn. I skipped so many classes that I finished the year with a near-failing grade point average (1.86 on a scale of 4.0, to be exact). Funny how I can remember my exact GPA after more than forty years. I felt guilty about wasting my parents' money. So, near the end of my first year of college, I joined the Navy without consulting Mom or Dad. I'll never forget the day I went home and told them the decision I had made. Mom cried, and Dad laughed, a knee-slapping, gut-busting, deep, roaring laugh. It took me quite a while to figure out the joke was on me, and Dad knew it from day one.

In 1972 I began four years of active duty in the Navy as a hospital corpsman. My second duty station was at Sigonella Naval Air Station near Catania, Sicily. While there I met another hospital corpsman named Susie Brunn, who was from the farmlands of northwest Ohio. She was pretty, engaging, and almost always happy. One day Susie was humming as she swabbed the deck in the dispensary. One of the petty officers asked what kind of drug Susie was taking to put her in such a good mood. The response was, "She's high on life." It was true. Susie was just happy to be there, wherever she was. I had traveled five thousand miles and met a young woman whose hometown was only two hundred miles from mine. Coincidence? I don't think so. It was a "God-incidence." According to God's plan, Susie became the most important person in my life, though I didn't know it at the time.

Living in southern Europe was the opportunity of a lifetime for me. I had never traveled before. The first time I flew on an airplane was to report to Navy boot camp when I was nineteen years old. I got to travel extensively around Europe twice. As fun as Sicily was though, I couldn't wait to get back home to the US of A, to the "real world," as I called it back then. It was time for me to make my mark on America, whatever that might be. Yet, two thoughts nagged me that I was able suppress but could not escape. Nothing I had tried on my own gave me lasting satisfaction, and I could still distinctly remember where Mom and Dad found their peace and joy. (More on the story of my search later.)

Something Fundamental Is Missing in America

After I was discharged from the Navy, it seemed to me that the America to which I had just returned was very different from the homeland I left two years earlier. Our country hadn't changed that much in two years. I simply noticed it more because I was seeing it through eyes that hadn't viewed daily life in America for several years. The changes were real, and with each passing year it became clear to me that the America I lived in was very different from the homeland I knew before. I understand that most things change with the passage of time, and every generation can make the same claim, but some things have remained the same. Whether forty years ago or today, Americans have lived, and continue to live, in one of the most powerful, influential, affluent countries on earth. Despite that, something basic seems to have changed. Something fundamental seems to be missing. Consider the following current trends.

- According to the Centers for Disease Control, American expenditures for prescription medications increased from $205.2 billion in 2005 to over $333.4 billion in 2017,[1] an increase of 62 percent in 12 years.
- The National Institute of Mental Health reported that in 2017, 4.5 percent of US adults (11 million) and 9.4 percent of US adolescents ages 12 to 17 (2.3 million) suffered from at least one major depressive episode with severe impairment of life activities.[2]
- Lisa J. Colpe, PhD, in an article called "Deaths of Despair: How Connecting Opioid Data Extends the Possibilities for Suicide Research" posted by the Centers for Disease Control and Prevention, reported, "Suicide, drug overdose, and alcohol-related deaths—known together as 'deaths of despair'—are increasing across the United States."[3] A chart embedded in this article, indicates, by my calculation, that deaths by suicide per 100,000 persons increased from 10.1 in 1999 to 14.3 in 2018; an increase of 40 percent in 20 years.

Gary Inrig, in his book *True North*, says, "Money is the 'god of this world,' and it empowers millions of people to enjoy life by living on substitutes. With money they can buy entertainment, but they can't buy joy. They can go to the drugstore and buy sleep, but they can't buy peace. Their money will attract a lot of acquaintances, but very few real friends. Wealth gains them admiration and envy, but not love. It buys the best medical services, but it can't buy health."[4]

Something is terribly wrong with this picture. As a Christian, I find it easy to understand something is missing from the life of non-believers. They don't have the love, joy, peace, and hope that believers have in Christ. Is this malady confined to the unsaved, or are Christ followers in America affected as well? In *Crazy Love*, Francis Chan says, "We all know something's wrong. At first I thought it was just me. Then I stood before twenty thousand Christian college students and asked, 'How many of you have read the New Testament and wondered if we in the church are missing it?' When almost every hand went up, I felt comforted. At least I'm not crazy."[5] Maybe the answer for Christians is not as clear as I once thought. It seems as if believers are also searching for something that is missing from their lives.

Human Needs

I tend to think of water, food, clothing, and shelter as the basic needs for human survival, but humans have additional fundamental needs if they are going to flourish rather than merely survive. Most of us want to be in relationship with others, to love and be loved, to be valued by others, to be considered significant by ourselves and others, and to add value to this life on earth. These topics have been discussed at length by sociologists, psychologists, self-help gurus, and others. Many articles and books address this topic as well. These desires are perfectly natural because God made us to be relational. His desire is for every person to seek an intimate relationship with him, so he can fulfill those needs.

Yet, he leaves the decision to us. We choose what determines success in our lives. We decide what is important and what we will worship. Make no mistake; we all worship something, a desire we place above all else. Few, if any, people worship golden calves in America, but many worship gold or other worldly treasures. What comes first in your life, God or self? Some common idols in America today include power, fame, and wealth. In essence, these are nothing more than varying aspects of self-worship. Could a question of purpose, or lack thereof, be plaguing Americans today more than ever?

Bringing Glory to God

God's plan doesn't involve our self-esteem or self-achievement. Instead, it calls for us to esteem others, to serve others, so God may receive glory from our deeds. God does not think as we think. As the Lord declared through the prophet Isaiah, "As the heavens are higher than the earth, so are my ways higher than your ways and my thoughts than your thoughts" (Isaiah 55:9). Nor does God value what humans' value. As the Lord was preparing to replace Saul as king of Israel, the prophet Samuel saw Eliab, son of Jesse, and believed Eliab was the man God would choose. But God told Samuel, "Do not consider his appearance or his height, for I have rejected him. The Lord does not look at the things people look at. People look at the outward appearance, but the Lord looks at the heart" (1 Samuel 16:7).

Our souls are more valuable to God than our worldly success, fame, or even our very lives. From a temporal perspective, we have several basic needs, but we only have one eternal need. God says the salvation of our souls is more valuable than the water we drink or the bread we eat. For what value is there in living if we die lost, without Christ? As Jesus told his disciples, "What good will it be for someone to gain the whole world, yet forfeit their soul? Or what can anyone give in exchange for their soul?" (Matthew 16:26). On another occasion, Jesus explained to his disciples how he was sustained by completing his Father's will. Jesus's life, and God's will, were inextricably intertwined. "My food," Jesus said, "is to do the will of him who sent me and to finish his work" (John 4:34). In one short sentence, Jesus encapsulated the purpose for everything he said and did while on earth.

What, then, is our purpose while living on this earth? Hundreds, if not thousands, of books have been written to address this question. Even more articles and sermons have been devoted to this topic. One might think this question would be easy for believers to answer since Christians have God's Word to provide answers, but is it? A couple of believers present their biblical views regarding God's purpose for our lives as follows.

- In the preface to his book, *Roaring Lambs*, Bob Briner highlights three significant professional events in his life, each time posing the same question, "What am I doing here?"[6] Bob continues, stating, "I am convinced that most Christians have no idea about the possibilities of being lambs that roar—of being followers of God who know how to fully integrate their commitment to Christ into their daily lives."[7] Bob concludes the preface, saying, "This book will recount more of opportunities missed than of opportunities taken. But I hope that even that will help you to take better advantage of your own daily opportunities to obey Christ's command to be salt and light in the world. I hope it will help you answer the question 'What am I doing here?' with steadfast assurance."[8]
- Rick Warren poses a single question in the title of his book, *The Purpose Driven Life—What on Earth Am I Here For?*[9] His book answers this question, explaining five biblical purposes for our lives.[10]

Earlier, I said I didn't understand why God would choose to place so many Christians in my life while I was engaged in willful, repetitive sin. To be more accurate, I do understand one reason why God would do such a thing. I am convinced God placed many Christians in my path both before and after I gave my life to Jesus Christ because he wanted to place me in the path of other souls, both saved and lost, to help them along this journey we call life. But this is only one aspect of God's purpose for my life.

According to God's plan, I am convinced my purpose in life is singular. Scripture says,

- "If anyone speaks, they should do so as one who speaks the very words of God. If anyone serves, they should do so with the strength God provides, so that in all things God may be praised through Jesus Christ. To him be the glory and the power for ever and ever. Amen." (1 Peter 4:11)
- "So, whether you eat or drink or whatever you do, do it all for the glory of God." (1 Corinthians 10:31)

I was created to bring glory, honor, and praise to Almighty God through Christ Jesus in everything I say and do. I exist because of him and for him (Hebrews 2:10). If you were to ask one hundred Christians, "What is God's single purpose for your life?," you would probably get many different answers. These might include: love God, love Jesus, go to church regularly, pray, witness to the lost, and care for widows and orphans in need, just to name a few. Each of those objectives are worthy endeavors if done in the name of Jesus Christ to bring glory to God, but all of these actions fall under a single purpose: bringing glory to God in everything we say and do.

Chapter 3

The Calling

As a prisoner for the Lord, then, I urge you to live a life worthy of the calling you have received. (Ephesians 4:1)

Once we understand God's singular purpose for our lives, by what path or process can we achieve this? Scripture addresses several callings extended by God to humankind. I will discuss three. They are the call to: 1) salvation, 2) holy living, and 3) specific ministry. The call to salvation is first since no other call will be extended to us until we have accepted Jesus Christ as our Lord and Savior. It is impossible for us to live holy lives or engage in ministry for the kingdom of heaven unless we are first followers of Christ.

The Call to Salvation—God's Plan of Redemption

If you were to ask someone to identify the two main parts of the Bible, they would likely say the Old and New Testaments. Another way we can identify two main parts in Scripture is theologically. Genesis 1–3 describes the creation and fall of humanity. The rest of the Bible, from Genesis 4 through to the end of Revelation, describes God's redemption of humankind or, stated another way, God's call to salvation. Those who don't know Scripture may ask, "Why do people need to be redeemed or saved?" That's a great question.

When God created Adam and Eve and placed them in the Garden of Eden, he instructed them not to eat of the tree of knowledge of good and evil.

However, they disobeyed by eating the fruit, resulting in sin and death entering the world. Because of their sin, every person is born with a sinful nature into a decaying world. Some may claim, "It's not fair for me to be penalized because Adam and Eve made the wrong choice." However, you could pick any one man and woman, place them in the Garden of Eden, and the result would have been the same. Human nature is flawed because it is self-centered, not God-centered. So, sin separates us from God, who is perfectly holy. Because of his love and mercy, God devised a plan of salvation, so we could be brought back into a right relationship with him. I call this plan grace. At just the right time, God sent his one and only Son Jesus Christ to earth as a human. Jesus lived a sinless life and then allowed himself to be nailed to a cross to die in our place for our sins.

By the death of Jesus, God's perfect, sinless lamb, the debt was paid for the sins of all people, satisfying God's holy requirement. At that moment, sin was conquered forever for those who believe in Jesus Christ. There has never been a sinless human other than Jesus who is able to pay the price for humanity. On the third day, God raised Jesus from the dead. At that moment, death was defeated forever. A short time later, Jesus ascended into heaven to be with God, his Father. One day Jesus will return to earth. Those who have accepted Jesus Christ as Lord and Savior, because of his sacrifice for them, will spend a glorious eternity with him. Those who do not accept Jesus as Lord and Savior will go to eternal torment. This is the basic message of the fall and redemption of humankind relayed to us in God's Word.

Those who have accepted God's call to salvation by accepting Jesus Christ as Lord and Savior understand exactly what those words mean. Some people reading these words may not have made such a decision yet. Such people, who are unfamiliar with Scripture and are searching for the answer to these questions in a single verse in the Bible, could become confused. I don't believe God's plan of salvation is fully contained within a single verse in Scripture. It requires multiple verses, taken in aggregate, to fully understand what God expects regarding his plan of salvation for us. How would you respond if a person asked, "What are the specific steps it takes for me to gain eternal life with Jesus Christ?" In Scripture I find four components or actions required to achieve eternal life through salvation.

- Belief—Believe in Jesus Christ, the Son of God, who died on the cross in our place to pay the debt for our sins and was raised to life on the third day, so we may have eternal life with him one day (John 20:31).
- Repentance—Repent of our sins (Luke 24:46–47), turning away from willful sin to live a life for Christ (1 John 2:5–6).
- Confession—Confess faith in Jesus Christ as our Savior and the Lord of our lives (Romans 10:9–10).
- Baptism—Be baptized (completely immersed or submerged in water) for the forgiveness of our sins and to receive the gift of the Holy Spirit (Acts 2:38).

It is important to note, immersion in water does not save us. The act of baptism merely symbolizes us dying to our old sinful life, being buried with our Savior Jesus Christ, and then being resurrected, raised to new life in Jesus Christ our Lord (Romans 6:3–5). We are saved by faith in the resurrected Christ, symbolized by baptism (1 Peter 3:21). The result of accepting Jesus Christ as Lord and Savior is a new creation, a new life as we bear much fruit for God's glory (John 15:4–8).

Those who believe in Jesus Christ as Lord and Savior first accepted God's Word as the one indisputable truth, for only in the Bible do we see Jesus Christ portrayed as God's sacrificial Lamb, our Lord, and Savior. However, the act of accepting Jesus Christ is not an end unto itself. It is a new beginning, a call to action. It is the first step, enabling us to be directed by the Holy Spirit to bring glory to God. To serve the living God, I must be cleansed of my sins by the blood of Jesus Christ (Hebrews 9:14). If I give every dollar I possess and every waking hour helping those in need yet do not do these things in the name of Jesus Christ, I only bring glory to me, not God.

My Call to Salvation—Finding My Purpose

When I first met Susie Brunn in Sicily, I had no idea she would become my wife. In fact, Susie told me she was never going to get married. With neither of us looking to get married, I was reminded of a saying: "This is a match made in heaven." It was but not for the reasons I thought. This introduction to Susie proved to be a huge turning point in my spiritual life. Unbeknownst to either of us, the Lord intended to utilize Susie in a significant way to bring me back to him.

THE CALLING

In the fall of 1976, Susie and I were discharged from the Navy and returned home, me to the hills of West Virginia and Susie to the farmlands of northwestern Ohio. In April 1977, Susie and I were wed.

Neither of us were Christians as we settled into married life in West Virginia. My priorities were getting an education, a good job, and a home. My conscious desire was for a career and possessions. I had a purpose, a worldly plan for my life, and I was going to put it into action. Then in 1979 God blessed us with our first child, a son. Susie was attending a non-denominational Christian church where, in June 1981, she accepted Jesus Christ as her Lord and Savior. I was working full time, attending college full time, and drinking full time on the weekends. Susie was the only Christian witness in our home, which desperately needed it. She served quietly and faithfully as the lone spiritual leader in our home for the next eleven years. Susie was a patient witness under difficult circumstances. Anyone who has lived as the lone Christian in a household knows exactly what I mean.

With the passage of time, I began to think (it was really Susie's thinking and her gentle prodding, but I like to take credit for good ideas anywhere I can) our children should be attending church services. They needed to be informed about matters of salvation and eternity, so they could make a proper decision about their faith at the appropriate time. But every time I started thinking about the Lord, I felt a heavy guilt about turning my back on him and living contrary to my upbringing. So, I resolved to put a new and better plan of action in place. In my infinite "wisdom," I decided to get my life in order first, then mend my relationship with the Lord. Little did I know I had just lost a major spiritual battle, and all of Satan's minions were giving me a standing ovation for such an "intelligent" decision.

I was attending church services with Susie. The congregation did what they could to befriend me and make me feel at home. During a revival, Dr. Harvey Bream, President of Cincinnati Bible College (now known as Cincinnati Christian University) came to speak. After the service one night, Dr. Bream came to our home to talk to me about God's plan of salvation and his plan for my life. I was mildly surprised that such an affluent and busy believer would make time to visit with me. During our conversation, I admitted I was lost, but I couldn't come to Christ until I had cleaned up my act. Dr. Bream was an articulate, persuasive man of God, but he couldn't convince me of the error in my thinking. The chains of guilt, shame, and pride continued to weigh me down. Little did I realize I had just lost another major spiritual battle. I had admitted two crucial flaws that I was lost and powerless to correct. I had played right into the devil's hands and was slowly drowning in my sin. Meanwhile, every crony of Satan was, once again, applauding another of my "wise" decisions.

If anyone would have told me I would leave West Virginia, I would have said they were crazy. Yet, after graduating from college in 1983, I took a job in Dayton, Ohio. Shortly thereafter, God blessed us with our second child, a daughter. We started attending a non-denominational church in the Dayton area, but I wasn't comfortable there at all. It seemed to me only a few people, two of whom were a couple named Gary and Cindy, really cared if I attended church services or not. Frankly, I considered attending there to be a waste of time. This was my perception and my problem, not the problem of that local body of Christ. What I saw as wasted time actually paid great dividends in the future. Again, little did I know that God had a plan for my life involving Gary and Cindy in a mighty way.

In 1986, God blessed us with our third and final child, a son. Meanwhile, Susie was praying for a church to open in our neighborhood, someplace closer to home and hopefully a place where I would feel more comfortable. In 1988, a church-planting group in the Dayton, Ohio, area decided to plant a church in our neighborhood in an old former school building. The pastor and his wife were none other than Gary and Cindy. Coincidence? I don't think so. It was a God-incidence. I had an instant connection through Gary and Cindy, and they wasted no time capitalizing on it.

Immediately, Gary found a job for me to do within the body of believers: shoveling coal into the furnace at the church building. Another important factor was the response of the congregation toward me. They accepted me "warts and all," as my dear mother would say. I was welcome among them even though I was not a Christian. Before long I was working in the church in other ways where they could use a non-Christian. Gary talked me into doing what he called a "small plumbing job" at the church building. It turned out to be not so small. (One thing has always puzzled me about preachers. They always seem to overestimate the crowd at service time and underestimate the amount of time it will take to complete the job they want others to do. But I digress). Gary and Cindy were determined to integrate me into the church family as soon as possible. Shoveling coal and plumbing jobs were two ways to accomplish this.

Bob and Sue were another couple in this local body of Christ. Gary and Cindy recruited them to help in their endeavors to lead me to the Lord. Bob and Sue became good friends with Susie and me. I fell in love with our church family because they loved me. I was devastated when, at the beginning of 1992, I learned this church body would disband in April. This body of believers had originally come together with the help of a two-year funding commitment by a church-planting group. At the end of the two years, it was clear the local congregation wasn't going to be able to sustain this church body and the building financially. I didn't know where I would go or what I would do. I felt like I was losing my home even though I wasn't a Christian.

The amazing thing to me was that the excellence in worship, preaching, and teaching did not lessen. No one coasted toward the final day. It was business as usual, worshipping the Lord, building up the existing Body of Christ, and wooing the lost. One morning before Sunday school started, I walked into one of the children's classrooms. As I stepped into the doorway of what I thought was an empty classroom, I heard and then saw Cindy standing in the far corner of the room with her back to the door. She was quietly crying as sobs shook her body. She was losing her family too. Her brothers and sisters in Christ would soon be going their separate ways, and there was nothing she could do about it. Her husband, Gary, the senior minister, was losing his congregation and his livelihood as well. But Cindy wasn't crying only for Christians. She was crying for the unsaved too, like me.

I backed out of the room quietly without Cindy realizing I had been there. But the man who backed out of the classroom was far different from the one who entered it. If I know anything about people, it is this: they do not willingly suffer for anything unless they truly believe in it. I was watching someone I knew, a genuine lover of Christ, who was suffering for her faith. She was in pain but would not quit or complain openly. In a few quiet seconds where no words were spoken, God used Cindy's humility and broken-heartedness to break my heart and override my guilt and shame. I can't tell you the day the Holy Spirit first started working on my wayward heart, but that Sunday morning, the Spirit began convicting me in earnest, and I knew it. My return to Jesus Christ was only a matter of time. Suddenly, the minions of hell were no longer applauding.

I still didn't know where I would go next. Again, unbeknownst to me (are you starting to see a pattern develop here?), Bob and Sue as well as Gary and Cindy were already plotting to find my next church home. Susie and I came up with a list of four or five churches to visit. Then Bob and Sue invited us to visit a church with them. I told Bob we had made plans to visit another church first. At this, Bob became uncharacteristically brusque with me. "No!" he said. "You come visit with me first and then visit those other churches later if you want." So, Susie and I went to church with Bob and Sue the next Sunday. I never went to visit another church. Little did I realize, Bob and Sue had already talked with the minister, Mike, and his wife, Suzy, to let them know we would be visiting. So, Mike and Suzy joined Bob and Sue and Gary and Cindy in their "heavenly conspiracy" to lead me to Christ.

Dave and Debbie were another couple we met quickly at our new church home. One Sunday morning I was sitting beside Debbie during worship service, and she noticed I didn't partake of communion as it was passed. I found out later that she started praying for me immediately. She knew I was either a Christian in trouble or a lost soul. Either way, I needed serious prayer. Susie and I became good friends with Dave and Debbie as well.

Meanwhile, my basic problem remained the same. I felt tremendous guilt for deserting the Lord. Still, I had enough false pride to think I could clean up my act before returning to him. I was stupidly allowing Satan to use no less than three paralyzing tools against me—guilt, shame, and pride—Instead of just one. On the human side, I was trying hard. My drinking lessened, I quit smoking, and I started cleaning up my language, but I was one miserable soul. That is not the most complimentary word to describe my interaction with the Holy Spirit, but it is perfectly true. If you've ever struggled mightily with the Spirit about something, you know what I mean. I was getting beat up regularly. God's Spirit was calling me one way, and the devil was pulling me the opposite way. I felt like a stretched rope in a tug of war, and I was about to snap. But I was steadfastly frozen in my indecision. Satan and his demons were once again celebrating because, in and of myself, I was beat. I was on a fast track to destruction, and I was, or at least I felt, helpless to stop it.

Bob asked if he could come to my house once a week for four weeks, so we could watch an evangelistic video series together. The last video was supposed to be the clincher. On the evening of Friday, October 16, 1992, Bob, my wife Susie, and I were sitting in our family room watching the next-to-last video when the Lord, in his infinite mercy, decided to intercede. God knew the desire of my heart and my utter weakness. He knew I was beaten and didn't have the willpower, strength, or intelligence to make the right decision alone. So, partway through the video, the Holy Spirit lifted the guilt from my shoulders. I am convinced God simply decided to show me, for just a few moments, what it would feel like not to carry guilt and shame anymore. It was wonderful. I felt such relief and joy. I went completely silent. Bob and Susie knew something was happening, but they weren't sure what. In their nervousness, they kept on jabbering. I can distinctly remember thinking, *You two need to shut up, so we can pray.* (I told them so later, and we had a good laugh about it). Soon they did grow silent, and I prayed the sweet prayer of repentance in the presence of my best friend and wife, Susie, and a very dear brother in Christ, Bob. I had just made the most important decision a human can make by accepting Jesus Christ as my Lord and Savior.

I called the senior minister, Mike, to let him know what had happened. On Sunday morning he asked if I was going to be baptized. I remembered Dad telling me about his mentor, brother Deward Jarrell, who once said, "Nolan [my dad], they can baptize you until the tadpoles know you by name, but that won't save you." So, I told Mike I didn't need to be baptized again since I had been baptized (immersed) into Christ when I was twelve years old. I could tell this disturbed him greatly. I said, "Mike, that really upsets you doesn't it?"

"Yes," he replied. "I think you ought to be baptized."

"OK. I'll meet you up front this morning, so you can baptize me," I said. "I'll come up every Sunday morning until you think we have it right."

Mike assured me that one time would be sufficient. So, I was immersed for a second time as I recommitted my life to Jesus Christ. I guess you could call me a spiritual "double dipper."

The story of my initial conversion and subsequent return to the Lord is not unique. In fact, I think it is common. Nor is my story particularly exciting, except to me and those who had been praying for me. I recount my long-winded story to remind you of several things we have in common and need to remember.

- I praise God for his relentless pursuit of me. Because of his great love for me, he displayed immense patience as he waited for my return to him. Truly, God's love and grace are far more lavish than I can fully understand.
- It is good for me to read my own confession and repentance. I need to remember where I was before I started my walk with the Lord, recalling the gutter of sin from which I was delivered. This is the best antidote for the poison of my pride.

- The third reason is my main impetus for including this story. When I was a young man, posters were everywhere of Uncle Sam pointing his finger and saying, "I want you." So does God. He wants every person to love him. He also wants to use every believer to help lead lost souls to him and build up those who already love him. People who love the Lord are his preferred tool for crafting eternity.

Look at the time, talent, and treasure of so many Christians God was willing to use to lead me back to him. That is God's love in action. In this part of my story alone, God used Mom, Dad, Susie, Dr. Bream, Gary, Cindy, Bob, Sue, Mike, Suzy, Dave, Debbie, and so many others. The people named are only the tip of the iceberg. Many others who are unnamed in these pages and even more who are unknown to me (prayer warriors, for example) were participants in my journey. As a member of God's family, he has a part for me to play in the lives of others if I am willing.

God's call to us, extending salvation to us through his grace, is the greatest gift we will ever receive on earth. Whether we accept this gift or not determines where we will spend eternity, but our salvation is not for eternity alone. It also determines the purpose for which we are to live each day.

The Call to Holy Living

Everyone who receives God's gift of salvation by accepting Jesus Christ as Lord and Savior is called to live a holy life (2 Timothy 1:9). God has called us to live our lives imitating Jesus Christ as best as we can, to be an example to the rest of the world regarding how humans should live. Because we belong to Jesus Christ, are in fellowship with him, and are obedient to him, we should see the world through Jesus's eyes, hear the world through his ears, and respond to the world as he would. The bottom line is this: those who love Jesus Christ are indwelt by God's Holy Spirit and will exhibit the fruit of his Spirit in their lives. They will do the best they can each day, relying on the Spirit to live as Jesus lived and as God's Word directs us.

How do we determine if we are living a life worthy of his calling? By what do we measure "worthy"? When Peter told the believers "for it is written: 'Be holy, because I am holy,'" he identified the person he was quoting: God Almighty (Leviticus 11:44–45). God is the only person whom the Old Testament identifies as worthy of praise. In the New Testament, Jesus Christ is also described as worthy of praise. "God was seated on the throne with a scroll in his right hand . . . No one in heaven or on earth was found worthy to open the scroll.. . . But the Lion of Judah, the Root of David, the Lamb of God was worthy to open the scroll . . . because he had been slain, and with his blood he purchased for God persons from every tribe and language and people and nation" (Revelation 5:1–9).

The measure we are to use to determine "worthy" is God Almighty and Jesus Christ, the precious lamb of God. In and of ourselves, we are hopelessly unworthy, but our hope is not in ourselves; it is in Christ. Thanks be to God Almighty, Jesus's sacrifice on the cross eliminated the requirement for humans to be perfect. We who claim Jesus Christ as Lord and Savior have been forgiven our sins because we are covered by the blood of God's sacrificial Lamb. Because of our faith in Jesus Christ as Lord and Savior, we "participate in his divine nature," and "his divine power has given us everything we need for a godly life," so we can "escape the corruption in the world caused by evil desires" (2 Peter 1:3–4). We are called to give our best effort to live a life for Christ daily. We can attain this goal with the Holy Spirit's help.

The Call to Specific Ministry

God has called us to salvation. Those who accept this extravagant gift are called to live a holy life, to bring glory to God through our lives. But God doesn't stop there because he is an intimate God. God knit me together in my mother's womb. He knows the number of hairs in my head. He made me, formed me, and created me for his glory (Isaiah 43:7). God knows me far more intimately than I know myself. Realizing God created me with such intimacy, it naturally follows he would have an intimately detailed plan for my life on earth as well. Paul called it "bearing fruit in every good work" (Colossians 1:10). However, God's plan for our individual lives is very particular, with specific words and deeds each of us are called to say and do at the time and place he ordains.

Throughout history God has placed specific individuals in precise locations at exact times to achieve a heavenly purpose. Many were chosen by God to give aid or witness to their fellow people in accordance with his plan. However, some were called to far more difficult ministries or situations. Here are a few examples of this from Scripture.

- God called Noah to build a colossal wooden ark in an arid land that may never have seen rain before, let alone a flood. The first rainfall recorded in Scripture is when the great flood started. Imagine the increasing ridicule Noah and his family must have endured as Noah's neighbors watched him construct the ark for nearly one hundred years. I can almost see some of Noah's neighbors gathering for lunch and entertainment as they watched Noah work on his boat in the desert and made jokes about his mental health.
- God gave Jonah a choice: go preach to the Ninevites, a people Jonah despised, or die.
- God chose Nehemiah to rebuild Jerusalem's wall while the workers were being attacked by enemies.
- God called Hosea to marry a promiscuous woman named Gomer and have children with her. When Gomer committed adultery after marrying Hosea, as God knew she would, God told Hosea to love Gomer as God loved the Israelites.
- God chose a young lady named Mary to be the mother of Jesus Christ. In the process, this virgin had to go tell her family and her betrothed she was pregnant, not by any human but by the Holy Spirit.
- God chose Rahab, a woman of ill repute living in Jericho, to risk her life by hiding two Israelite spies in her house, protecting them from the king of Jericho.

These people were placed in difficult or life-threatening positions by accepting God's call. Each person was chosen and directed by God, except for Rahab. I am convinced she was chosen by God and placed in Jericho for this specific purpose. However, God's Word gives us no indication he instructed Rahab regarding what she should do. By God's providential hand and through no circumstances of her own making, Rahab was thrust into a difficult situation. God knew what Rahab would do even before she decided it. By faith Rahab made the right decision, as did all the others. The Lord also assigns tasks to every believer in every generation. In many cases these assignments are neither dangerous nor publicized, but they are vital to the kingdom of heaven. Christians today are no different. Before the beginning of time, God planned specific tasks for each of us to accomplish for his glory.

Chapter 4

Our Role in God's Plan

"For I know the plans I have for you," declares the Lord, "plans to prosper you and not to harm you, plans to give you hope and a future." (Jeremiah 29:11)

I have heard different people, mostly televangelists, say God spoke to them, like he spoke to the patriarchs and prophets in ages past. God can certainly communicate with humans today as he did thousands of years ago, if he so desires. I can say I have never heard God speak directly to me, either in my ear or in my head, giving me a specific instruction, or calling me to a ministry, place, or event. I am not saying the Lord has never spoken, or tried to speak, to me, but if he tried, I did not hear him. Without a doubt, God has used his Word, the counsel of trusted Christians, and my circumstances to communicate with me. Regarding my calling from God, I'm in the same boat as Rahab, so to speak. So, how do I properly determine my role in God's plan?

It's Not Our Plan

For starters, let's keep first things first. Lest we forget; it's not our plan. It's God's plan. Our role in God's plan is clearly defined.

Before time was created or humans were formed, the decision was finalized regarding how sinful people would be reconciled to a Holy God.

- God devised the plan.
- Jesus provided the path.
- The Holy Spirit provided the power.
- We are called to proclaim.

As sinful humans, we are inconsequential, insignificant in making God's plan of redemption succeed. Let me be clear: every human is extraordinarily significant to God, but humans cannot make God's plan succeed any more than they can make God's plan fail. God's plan of redemption cannot fail because its success was perfectly achieved through a resurrected Christ some two thousand years ago. Therefore, it is important for each of us to understand what we can and cannot do for the kingdom of heaven.

- We cannot save the lost. Only Jesus's death, burial, and resurrection can save the lost. However, we can point others to Jesus, the only one who can save.
- We cannot forgive a person's sins enabling them to receive salvation. (We can only forgive a sin someone commits against us). We can seek lost souls and introduce them to the one who redeems, Jesus, who can forgive sins.
- We cannot reform society's morals. However, we can reform our morals once the Holy Spirit takes up residence within us. We can also attempt to influence the morals of other humans by making Jesus known to them.
- We cannot convict or convince others of their sins. Only God's Spirit can accomplish this.
- We are not allowed to add to, subtract from, or otherwise change God's Word. We can impart God's Word and point people toward Jesus, the living word.
- We are not allowed to craft or negotiate God's message to the world. We simply proclaim the good news given to us and point everyone to Jesus Christ.

Trumpets played a significant role in the life of the Israelites. They were used for several purposes at God's direction. A primary purpose was to announce his presence. Our primary role while engaging the world is to proclaim God's love and his plan of salvation through Jesus Christ. We are God's modern-day trumpets, his heralds, one of his conduits of communication. Realizing what we cannot achieve for the kingdom should liberate us to concentrate on those areas of ministry we can achieve. Understanding our limited role in God's plan frees us from the burden of attempting to accomplish the impossible, even if we think we should be able to do so. It is not humans but the triune God who convicts, redeems, reforms, and transforms. We can divide the roles of ministry into three broad categories: planting, watering, and growing. As humans we can plant and water, but only God Almighty can make salvation "grow."

How do you plant? How do you water? What specific ministry area is the best fit for you to serve the Lord effectively? God's Word says, "There are different kinds of gifts, but the same Spirit distributes them. There are different kinds of service, but the same Lord. There are different kinds of working, but in all of them and in everyone it is the same God at work" (1 Corinthians 12:4–6).

Spiritual Gifts

Through his Spirit, God has given spiritual gifts to all who believe in Jesus Christ. These heavenly presents are given to believers to assist them in their ministry. Each Christian is responsible to identify the gifts bestowed upon them by the Holy Spirit. The godly endowments we have received are not the only consideration in determining what type of service is best for us. God shaped each of us exactly as he desired. He created us with certain interests, abilities, a unique personality, and then ensured we gained specific life experiences. Why does this matter? Because God shaped each of us, so we would flourish in specific ministries when he calls us. For example, if a believer's primary spiritual gift is service, and the person is shy and uncomfortable with attention, maybe God didn't intend for the person to engage in public speaking. Such a person is probably best suited to engage in one-on-one or small group relationships or serving "behind the scenes." We all know devoted servants like this.

But what if someone doesn't realize the spiritual gift(s) they have received from God's Spirit? Numerous assessments are available to help Christians identify these gifts. I am certain your minister, an elder, or other mature Christian friend will be happy to help you find the proper assessment to determine the spiritual gift(s) you possess. Once you have identified the ministry area(s) best suited to you and get engaged, you should be able to serve effectively and enthusiastically within your local body of Christ. As you serve, listen for God's voice, diligently attempting to discern the leading of the Holy Spirit as he guides you to those specific persons and places where he wants you to be.

God has used humans as his messenger throughout most of the history of humankind. God spoke to his people through the patriarchs, Moses, Joshua, the judges, prophets, and priests. Then John the Baptist heralded the coming Christ. While Jesus was engaged in public ministry, he went from town to town announcing the good news of the kingdom. After Jesus ascended to heaven, the apostles took up the mantle, proclaiming the good news of the kingdom. All these people served as God's mouthpieces to make his message known to the world. Likewise, believers today are called to proclaim God's message, salvation through faith in Jesus Christ.

Chapter 5

The Struggle Against Self

> For in my inner being I delight in God's law; but I see another law at work in me, waging war against the law of my mind and making me a prisoner of the law of sin at work within me. (Romans 7:22–23)

Those who are committed to living their lives for Christ, bringing glory to God, will face a number of obstacles. To succeed, we must overcome our sinful nature, the sinful of humankind, and Satan. The next five chapters outline these struggles, starting with ourselves.

Those who love the Lord are called to proclaim the good news of the kingdom of heaven. As we go through life heralding faith in Jesus Christ, we are called to live as he did. God knew this would be impossible for us before he called us. He doesn't expect perfection from us. He desires that we strive for perfection. No matter how much we love the Lord, all of us have human frailties. I carry my baggage with me everywhere I go. It contains any number of items, including sin, pride, guilt, shame, doubt, illness, and mortality, to name a few. As we live for our Lord, these flaws can be distracting at the very least and debilitating at times. Fortunately, God has provided us with an extraordinarily powerful aid, the indwelling Holy Spirit, to shore up our human deficiencies.

An Honest Assessment

An honest self-assessment, as mentioned earlier, is one tool all believers can utilize to maintain and improve their walk with the Lord. We need to view ourselves regularly in the mirror of God's Word to determine the status of our progress. Because of our fallen nature, the need for improvement never ends on earth. Self-assessment can be a difficult task since the reflection in the mirror may not be very pretty. If I decide to delay a self-examination by saying, "I'm good just as I am," I am deluding myself. If I say, "I'm doing the best I can," I am usually attempting to delay the process of self-improvement rather than stating the truth.

Please understand this is not about laying a guilt trip on anyone. I've had guilt trips laid on me by what I presumed to be well-intentioned Christians. I didn't like it, and I won't do it to you. I am, and continue to be, a flawed human. I struggle with "self" every day to walk in faith. After more than twenty-eight years of walking with Jesus, I continue to be a work in progress. The Holy Spirit still has much more to accomplish in me. My default position regarding those who love Jesus is they have a strong desire to make a positive, eternal difference while on earth. Our self-assessments, while difficult at times, will allow us to improve who we are, what we do, and how we do it, with the help of God's Spirit. If we allow him to show us the areas that need improvement, we have done a good thing. If we then choose to work diligently to correct the flaws, we have done an even better thing, taking another step toward becoming the people God intends us to be. The Holy Spirit is waiting and willing to help us in this endeavor. Furthermore, it's not as though our introspection will surprise God. Before the world began, he knew every flaw in each of us, but he still created us and then sent his Son to die for us.

The Full Armor of God

The devil, armed with powerful weapons of war, is a daunting foe to lost souls who have no spiritual protection. Unlike lost souls, we, as soldier's in the Lord's army, are protected as we engage in spiritual battle. Those who love the Lord are called to stand strong in his mighty power by donning the full armor of God, which consists of the following:

- The belt of truth
- The breastplate of righteousness
- Feet fitted with the readiness that comes from the gospel of peace
- The shield of faith
- The helmet of salvation
- The sword of the Spirit, which is the Word of God (Ephesians 6:13–17)

Let's consider several things about the armor of God. The first part of the armor listed is truth, which is Satan's primary target in his war for human souls. Second, our only offensive weapon is the sword of the Spirit. Paul stated it in a slightly different way in his letter to the Christians in Corinth when he said, "As servants of God we commend ourselves . . . in truthful speech and in the power of God; with weapons of righteousness in the right hand and in the left (2 Corinthians 6:4, 7). While this weapon may very well be offensive (insulting) to those who are lost and dying, it is not to be used as an offensive weapon in the traditional human sense, to hurt or kill. In fact, the opposite is true. It is designed to enlighten and give life. Third, the armor of God is not designed to protect the soldier's back. The only parts of the armor touching the back side of a soldier are the helmet and the belt. The armor itself dictates a simple, clear battle tactic. We are called to face the enemy, stand firm, and prevail. When we resist the devil, he will flee from us, at least temporarily.

Human Chinks in the Armor of God

Those who are indwelt by the Holy Spirit and are fitted with the armor of God are still vulnerable. Because of our sinful human nature and decaying bodies, we create chinks in the armor, areas of weakness where Satan will return to attack again. We have varying degrees of control over these flaws. Two examples where we have limited control are illness and disease. There are other human frailties where we can exert a lot of control. Let's look at three areas of weakness where we can make improvements. They are self-centeredness, utilization of time, and our level of engagement for the kingdom of God as we walk this earth.

Increasing Self-Centeredness

Self-centeredness seems to be increasing with each passing decade in our country. Mom and Dad's generation spent their earliest years in the Great Depression and then went on to fight in World War II or support the war effort at home through sacrificial living. Many Americans, myself included, consider them as our "Greatest Generation" because of their servant hearts. I am part of a markedly different generation, the "Baby Boomers." As a teenager in the 1960s, many people of my generation discovered themselves, their rights, and their desires rather than sacrifice for their country. Self-discovery and self-gratification were significant motivating factors.

An article in 2008 by Pew Center Research, "Baby Boomers: The Gloomiest Generation," reports, "America's baby boomers . . . are more downbeat about their lives than are adults who are younger or older. Not only do boomers give their overall quality of life a lower rating than adults in other generations, they also are more likely to worry that their incomes won't keep up with inflation—this despite the fact that boomers enjoy the highest incomes of any age group."[1]

An article in 2014 by Paul Taylor, "More Than Half of Millennials Have Shared a 'Selfie,'" posted by Pew Research Center observes, "Millennials . . . have grown up with the new digital technologies of the 21st century. They're the heaviest users of the internet, cell phones and social media sites . . . 55% of Millennials have posted a 'selfie' on a social media site; no other generation is nearly as inclined to do this. Overall, 26% of Americans have shared a "selfie" on a photo-sharing or social networking site."[2]

A 2020 article by Pew Research staffers Amanda Barroso, Kim Parker, and Jesse Bennett, "As Millennials Near 40, They're Approaching Family Life Differently Than Previous Generations," states, "Millennials have been slower than previous generations to establish their own households . . . Millennials trail previous generations at the same age across three typical measures of family life: living in a family unit, marriage rates and birth rates."[3]

These observations, which are designed to show one significant pattern developing over three generations, could lead a person to conclude that each subsequent generation of Americans is moving away from serving others to serving self and even glorifying self.

Increasing Demands on Time

In the late 1970s and early 1980s, I was working in the warehouse of a discount store chain. It was there I saw, for the first time, the installation of a mainframe computer in a business. I was witnessing the introduction of technology into businesses that was supposed to revolutionize every industry and my life as well. Magazine and newspaper articles raved about how computers would make business operations more efficient, reducing the average work week to thirty-five hours or less. My experience has proven the opposite to be true. In 1984 I landed the job I would hold for the next twenty-six years, where I ended up working a minimum of fifty hours a week. As the years passed, business management increasingly tried to demand more of my time.

Consider this scenario. They are downsizing at work due to budgetary constraints, and you've inherited some additional tasks. The boss isn't happy you haven't completed the insanely long list of projects. The kids have marching band, chorus, and practice for whatever sport is in season. So, you take them to practices and attend all the events you can. Your church offers programs and events for every season and age group. Your children (up to a certain age) want you to spend more time with them (which is important). After a certain age, they would rather you just stay away (in which case your opportunity has passed). Your spouse says you two don't spend enough time alone (and it's true). Your parents haven't seen too much of you lately (and you feel guilty about it). Oh, and in your spare time, start working on the to-do list you've been ignoring, like cleaning out the garage. Whether it's reality or just my perception, it appears as if this merry-go-round we call "life" is spinning ever faster. Sound familiar?

Brett and Kate McKay, in an article called "The Eisenhower Decision Matrix," summarized Eisenhower's decision principle, stating, "What is important is seldom urgent and what is urgent is seldom important . . . The difference is, urgent tasks shouts 'Now,' requiring immediate attention and placing one in a reactive, defensive mode. Important tasks contribute to the long-term mission and goals, allowing one to operate in a calm, responsive mode . . . Spend more time on important tasks."[4]

Sometimes we confuse importance and urgency, thinking all things urgent are also important, when they usually aren't. I've seen work situations where someone presents a "false urgency," usually in the form of a short, arbitrary deadline for a project completion. I have also seen a worker who, attempting to get help on a matter, would present the issue to the manager as important and urgent when it wasn't. One manager I had, when confronted with such a situation, would respond with an insightful observation, saying, "A lack of planning on your part does not create an emergency on my part."

Time is a limited, precious resource. We don't know the amount allotted to us. Even while operating as efficiently as possible, the pace of life still makes me dizzy if I allow it. This plays right into the hands of Satan, who wants me running at warp speed continually. "You can do it," he whispers in my ear. "Just try a little harder. You can be the man of the year at work, church, and home." If I listen to such destructive advice, I become distracted and tired, make poor decisions, and operate inefficiently at best. At worst, eventually, I crash and burn. When I burn out, it impacts every aspect of my life. Busyness is a powerful instrument that the devil carries in his toolbelt. It seems to be particularly effective on Americans. Does he whisper in your ear as he does mine?

Fortunately, most of us know our limitations regarding the use of time and energy. Still, Satan takes every opportunity to promote busyness and distraction in us, even when we are trying to do good things. Martha was being a model host by making the necessary preparations for Jesus and his disciples when they visited her home. However, her focus on the preparations distracted her from making the better choice. She chose what was urgent rather than what was important.

What does Scripture identify as the most important matter? Jesus was asked, "Of all the commandments, which is the most important?" His answer was, "'Love the Lord your God with all your heart and with all your soul and with all your mind and with all your strength.' The second is this: 'Love your neighbor as yourself.' There is no commandment greater than these" (Mark 12:28–31). As we develop our relationship with the Lord through prayer and studying his Word, we are resting in him. We desperately need God's love and his rest to prepare ourselves to go into the world and love our neighbors. At times I'm a legend in my own mind. I like to think I can be everywhere and do everything, but the hard truth is, I can't. Whether I want to admit it or not, I need rest. The older I get, the more rest I need. Furthermore, rest is the perfect prescription for a life lived at warp speed.

At the beginning of this book, we talked about examining ourselves by looking in the mirror of God's Word. Paul did and told us what he saw. He presented a dark picture of himself, a scathingly frank assessment of his wretched, sinful nature. While Paul was speaking of himself, I am certain he knew he was not alone among humans in this regard. Fortunately, God ensured Paul gave us a silver lining to this dark cloud as well. At the end of this brutally honest assessment, Paul posed a single question: "Who will rescue me from this body that is subject to death?" Then he provided the answer, "Thanks be to God, who delivers me through Jesus Christ our Lord (Romans 7:24–25).

We are commanded to live a life of obedience and spread the good news, but loving God is the most important matter and our greatest calling. God knew if we adhered to this most important matter, then loving our fellow people, the second most important matter, would follow. God also knew these two loves would motivate us to achieve all the urgent spiritual matters as well, in his good time.

A Desire to Go Home—Oh Lord, Come Quickly

When Mom and Dad's fiftieth wedding anniversary approached, my brother, sister, and I decided to do something special for them. We planned for almost a year, searching for their dearest friends, relatives, and special people in their lives. The most amazing thing was, we kept this surprise party a secret. So, on Mom and Dad's anniversary, through subterfuge, we were able to lead them into a banquet hall filled with their loved ones. The first minute of the party made all the preparations worthwhile. As Mom and Dad entered the hall, they froze in the doorway. For the first time in my life, I saw my Dad totally speechless. You would have to know my Dad to appreciate the significance of such a reaction. He stood in silence as he scanned the room, looking from face to face. The people were cheering and clapping. Finally, Dad broke into laughter as he and Mom started walking around shaking hands and hugging people. Later, Dad told me he was shocked because he had never been in a crowd in public where every single face belonged to a dear loved one. Imagine what it's going to be like for us in heaven.

It is good for believers to relish the anticipation of eternity in a perfect home. It seems the longer I live on earth, the more I want to see heaven. I love the earth God created for me; it's a beautiful place, but it cannot compare to heaven. We can only imagine, quite feebly, the beauty, peace, and joy awaiting us in God's eternal abode. Another reason I long for heaven is because life on earth is hard. It's a long, grueling road trip. Those last few miles of the trip always seem to take the greatest amount of time. If the Lord blesses us with a full life on earth, we will live to see loved ones get sick or hurt and eventually die. If we live long enough, we too may suffer from debilitating illness or injury before we die. Mom started having significant health issues in her forties, which only increased over time. As she got older, Mom told me on numerous occasions, "Getting old isn't for sissies." How right she was. God Almighty holds Mom and Dad's spirits in his hands now. I have other relatives and dear friends who have departed earth and are also with the Lord. Their presence in heaven makes it even more precious to me.

Long before their fiftieth wedding anniversary, Mom and Dad awaited the return of Jesus Christ with anticipation. For decades Mom had a favorite fork she used all the time when eating. Many years ago, she made it perfectly clear to the family that no one was to ever get rid of "her" fork. Then Mom told us a story about a woman and her fork. This story, "Keep Your Fork," can be found on numerous websites and has been attributed to several different authors, but I heard the story first from Mom. A dying woman asked her preacher to be sure she was buried with her fork in her right hand. When the pastor expressed his puzzlement, the woman explained, "In all my years of attending church socials and potluck dinners, I always remember when the dishes of the main courses were being cleared, someone would inevitably lean over and say, 'Keep your fork.' It was my favorite part because I knew something better was coming. So, I just want people to see me in the casket with a fork in my hand and I want them to wonder, 'What's with the fork?' Then I want you to tell them: 'Keep your fork. The best is yet to come.'" Mom went to meet her Lord in November 2012, and her body was laid to rest with her fork in her hand.

I long for the day when Jesus returns to earth to claim his own. I want to see him face to face. I also want to see Mom and Dad again. Mom will smile sweetly as she gives me a soft hug and a kiss. Dad will laugh boisterously as he gives me a bear hug and a kiss. And we will never, ever be separated again.

Mom, Dad, and my cousin Suzy met every week with friends at Paul and Ruth's house for Bible study and communion. Paul loved the Lord and usually led the devotion time. He was also convinced the Lord was going to allow him to remain alive to see Christ return, but Paul got sick and became weaker as time passed. His greatest disappointment was the realization he would probably die before the Lord's return, which he did. The desire of Paul's heart was to live to see his Lord return and eternity to begin.

It's not only people on earth who long for the Lord to return quickly. Some in heaven want to see the Lord return quickly to earth as Judge. As

John the Revelator tells us, when the fifth seal was opened, the souls of the martyrs under the altar called out to the Lord asking how long it would be until the Lord would judge the inhabitants of the earth and avenge their blood (Revelation 6:9–11). We must not try to get ahead of God Almighty as we await our Savior's return. God alone knows the exact day and hour when he will send Jesus back to us.

Self-centeredness, daily demands on our time, and a desire to see eternity can all detract us from completing the tasks God has assigned to us. In these last days as we await our Savior's return, we should be diligently pursuing God's plan, bringing glory to him by living self-controlled lives, encouraging the body of believers, and helping lead lost souls to Jesus.

CHAPTER 6

The Struggle with the Word of God

> For the word of God is alive and active. Sharper than any double-edged sword, it penetrates even to dividing soul and spirit, joints, and marrow; it judges the thoughts and attitudes of the heart. (Hebrews 4:12)

Owner's Manual for Humans

I consider the Holy Bible my guidebook, God's "owner's manual" for me. It is a miraculous wonder to me, unlike any other book known to humanity because it is living, active, and able to judge the thoughts and attitudes of the heart. This is not some kind of magic or trickery. God's Word accomplishes this by the power of the Holy Spirit. With regularity, the Bible speaks to my spirit, revealing a truth or convicting me of something. On more than one occasion, a familiar passage of Scripture has spoken to me as it never had before. It was as if God knew my need at that moment and addressed that need through those particular verses as I read them. I have also been listening to a sermon when God decided to use the minister's words to speak directly to a need I had right then. The minister was unaware of my need, but God was not. It seems to be so because it is so. The Spirit of God spoke to me to guide me. Therein lies the power of the Word of God, either spoken or read, which makes it alive, active, and able to judge.

As I study the Bible, God may speak to me in a certain manner on a particular passage and later speak in a different manner on the same verses. However, these differing messages, tailored to my needs at that moment, are always complementary, never contradictory, to the rest of the Bible. It's like looking at light through a prism. As I change the angle of the prism, the sunlight I see may be blue, red, or yellow, but the source of light is constant, the same. Likewise, the Spirit God refracts his Word to enlighten me regarding what I need to understand right then. What a miracle we have sitting on our coffee table, nightstand, or bookshelf.

Among those who love Jesus, some hold varying beliefs regarding the inerrancy of God's Word and his plan of salvation. I believe these are two of the most fundamental Christian issues that are presented in Scripture in a straightforward manner. So, why are there differing opinions within the Body of Christ regarding these issues? I can think of only two reasons why anyone would adopt an errant position as a basis for their actions in life and their expectations of eternity. Either they are truly mistaken in their belief or they have chosen to deceive themselves because their flawed reasoning is more convenient to accept than the truth. Let's look at three fallacies (as I believe them to be) that are contrary to the teaching of Scripture.

The Holy Bible We Have Today is not the Inerrant Word of God

A Barna Group article, "The End of Absolutes: America's New Moral Code," released in May 2016, made two interesting observations regarding truth.[1]

- Forty-one percent of practicing Christians agree the only truth one can know is whatever is right for one's own life.
- Fifty-nine percent of practicing Christians believe moral truth is absolute.

I was mildly shocked by how many within the Body of Christ said absolute moral truth does not exist. Then questions flooded into my head. If God's Word isn't the absolute truth for Christians, then what is? How can I be certain I am saved, that God's plan of salvation detailed in Scripture is true? How can I know the way I am supposed to live my life? How can I be sure heaven exists? Why should I tell anyone they need Jesus Christ as their Lord and Savior if I'm not convinced of my own salvation?

It is important for me to tell you my position on some basic biblical principles. I believe:

- There is one God, the creator of the heavens, earth, and everything in them.
- God created everything by his spoken word, from nothing, in six literal twenty-four-hour days.
- The Holy Bible is God's infallible Word, penned by human scribes, not of their own volition but as they were led by the Holy Spirit.
- Anything contrary to Scripture is false.
- I take the Holy Bible literally unless Scripture tells me the passage is figurative or a literal interpretation of the passage would contradict other passages in Scripture.
- The Holy Bible contains everything a person needs to understand how to attain eternal life with God and how we are to live on earth.
- Some passages in Scripture are figurative rather than literal. Mary's virgin birth, and Jesus's death, burial, resurrection, and ascension are not figurative.
- A great flood did cover the entire earth for months. wiping out all but eight humans.
- Hell, a place of eternal torment, was created by God Almighty for unrepentant humans just as certainly as he created an eternal paradise for those who love him.
- Figurative passages in Scripture do not negate, alter, or contradict the literal passages in Scripture.

I have had conversations with believers who accept parts of the Bible as true but deny the literal nature or reliability of certain portions of Scripture. I have heard at least two theories proposed by Christians regarding why they don't believe the Holy Bible, in its entirety, is the authoritative, flawless Word of God. The first theory goes something like this. God's Word was correct and authoritative when he first gave it to humankind. However, people have copied God's Word over and over and translated it time and again from one language to another, losing some of the accuracy of the translation in the process. Furthermore, it was not God but humans, a group of men, who chose the sixty-six books to be included in the King James Version of the Holy Bible.

The second theory says some passages in the Bible are fictional, earthly stories with a heavenly or spiritual meaning, similar to parables. The underlying stories are not literal but contain a heavenly or spiritual message that God wants to convey to us. Some of the passages in the Bible that could be included in this category are: a place of eternal torment, hell, created by an all-loving God for unrepentant humans, and many of the miraculous events recorded in Scripture.

So, how do we address these claims about Scripture? The Bible tells us repeatedly about some of the attributes of God Almighty including:

- He is all-powerful (Matthew 19:26).
- He is all-knowing (John 16:30).
- He is eternally loving (Psalm 136:1).
- He wants everyone to be saved (1 Timothy 2:4).
- He gave us his word to guide us into eternal life (John 8:51).
- He is vengeful. He will avenge himself against those who deny the gift of grace offered to us by the blood of Jesus Christ (Hebrews 10:29–31).

These are foundational biblical teachings about some of God's attributes. If any one of these attributes is not true, how can anything else in Scripture be relied on as true? An all-powerful God who created everything out of nothing by his spoken word, who will one day change our perishable bodies into imperishable bodies, who raised Jesus from the dead after three days, and who will take us to live with him eternally in heaven one day is certainly able to ensure we were given the proper instructions (the Holy Bible), so we could gain eternal life with him. If God is not powerful enough to ensure we were given the proper instructions, how can he be powerful enough to accomplish the other feats attributed to him in Scripture?

Some may say they believe God is powerful enough to ensure humans were given the proper instructions but decided, for some reason, to allow humans to misinterpret or distort Scripture. The "logic" behind this reasoning is, God allows humankind to sin in many other ways every day. After all, we have varying versions of the Bible that have different numbers of books.

What a cruel trick it would be if Almighty God could have given us the proper instructions to gain eternal life yet chose to allow us to be given an incorrect instruction book, thereby leading us away from eternal life with him. Such an action or omission would contradict the passages in Scripture that tell us God wants everyone to come to repentance.

Earlier I mentioned how easy it is for me to delude myself, particularly when it helps me meet one or more of my basic needs. When I need to be right, one of the ways I can try to accomplish this is to search Scripture for verses to help me "prove" my point on a given topic. When I do this, it is easy for me to take a verse out of context and misinterpret its meaning. Such logic is skewed, inconsistent, and usually erroneous.

We have all heard or participated in conversations regarding whether a particular verse in the Bible is literal or figurative. On several occasions I have heard a Christian say a portion of Scripture is not literal and simply did not happen. Most times such a conclusion relates to a miraculous event. On another occasion, the same believer will quote something as true, citing the Internet as the source of authority. Such skewed logic mystifies me. I marvel at this in an exasperated way. Anyone can put almost anything on the Internet. Many times, these authors are anonymous. Even if the author is known, no one is verifying the accuracy of these posted articles or stories. I've seen articles on the Internet regarding recent sightings of Elvis Presley and alien abduction of humans who were subsequently returned to earth.

We would all do well to remember the Internet contains many articles and stories, some of which are erroneously claiming to be factual. Others are opinions presented as proven facts, and still others are outright hoaxes to see who will take the bait. If we are trying to find the truth, we need to consistently apply the criteria we have established for determining if a statement is reliable and correct. Where is the consistency, the logic, in believing what someone has placed on the Internet and then questioning the accuracy or reliability of Scripture? Where is the logic or consistency in believing God will take some or all people to heaven but not believing in hell when Scripture speaks of both places repeatedly? If you build a house on a flawed foundation, it will crumble under pressure. Let's look at two major cracks in a foundation built on anything other than God's Word alone.

Grace and Works—A Flawed Theology

Americans have a reputation for being hard-charging, self-sufficient, goal-oriented people. Many, if not most of us, want a definitive yardstick, a concrete means by which to measure our success compared to others in this world. I have a dear friend who sometimes talks with me about spiritual matters. My friend, who believes in God Almighty and the saving grace of his Son, Jesus Christ, has stated several times, "I hope I've done enough to get into heaven." My friend, and some other believers I know, acknowledge the grace extended to them by God Almighty is a gift. Yet, they seem inclined to rely on a combination of grace and works as the measure to determine if they will attain an eternal abode in heaven. God's Word tells us it is impossible to earn our way into heaven.

This erroneous plan of salvation by a combination of faith and works has been taught since Jesus walked on earth. In his Word, God has presented his plan of salvation to redeem humanity from sin and death. This plan of redemption is why Jesus Christ left heaven, wrapped himself in flesh and bone, walked this earth, was tempted in every way yet lived a sinless life, allowed himself to be nailed to a cross in our place for our sins, and was resurrected by the Father on the third day, having defeated sin and death forever. Faith in Jesus Christ as Lord and Savior is the only path to the Father.

Jesus reserved some of his harshest words for those who willingly teach falsely regarding God's plan of salvation for humankind. The Pharisees and the Sadducees, who studied the Mosaic Law knew a Messiah was coming and how they were supposed to lead God's people. Jesus chastised these teachers of the law, publicly exposing them as hypocrites and blind guides because they were arrogant people who loved human praise and burdened the people with human rules and regulations while ignoring God's law. Jesus summed up the result of the Pharisees' ministry under the law in unequivocal terms: "Woe to you, teachers of the law and Pharisees, you hypocrites! You travel over land and sea to win a single convert, and when you have succeeded, you make them twice as much a child of hell as you are" (Matthew 23:15).

Also, during the early days of the church, certain teachers of the law told new converts to Christianity that unless they were circumcised according to Moses's law, they could not be saved (Acts 15:1, 5). The ruling religious Jews of Jesus's day also rejected the Messiah's presence although they knew, or should have known, the prophecies concerning his coming. Even if they did not immediately realize Jesus of Nazareth was the Messiah, they should have been able to put two and two together as they saw the miracles he performed in the name of God and the Old Testament prophecies he fulfilled. Jesus even forgave sins in their presence. The religious leaders also knew Jesus claimed to be the Messiah. Yet, before and after Jesus was crucified, buried, and resurrected, they were "hell-bent" on continuing to preach and teach that God's plan of salvation was through strict observance of Mosaic law and their interpretation of it.

Paul, in contrast, consistently preached salvation came by faith in the crucified, resurrected Christ, a salvation of grace through faith, not by works. Paul spent significant time and effort correcting the false teaching regarding salvation by a combination of works and grace. He understood the differences between and the eternal consequences of living under the law and living under grace. Paul also understood that under grace, circumcision was no longer a matter of the flesh but of the heart.

This was a huge salvation issue in the first century, and it still is today. In his letter to the Christians in Galatia, Paul explains that works and grace cannot go together regarding God's plan of salvation. They are mutually exclusive. Trying to mix works and grace is akin to mixing oil and water. Through the Holy Spirit's guidance, Paul succinctly compared the law and grace when he wrote, "Those who rely on faith are blessed . . . All who rely on the works of the law are under a curse . . . No one who relies on the law is justified [declared or made right with God], because the righteous will live by faith. The law is not based on faith" (Galatians 3:9–12). To add maximum emphasis to salvation by grace through faith as the only way to the Father, as Paul wrote, "I am astonished that you are so quickly deserting the one who called you to live in the grace of Christ and are turning to a different gospel . . . But even if we or an angel from heaven should preach a gospel other than the one we preached to you, let them be under God's curse" (Galatians 1:6, 8).

In addition to the previous passages, other verses contrast grace and works, including the following:

- James tells us when God gave his law to Moses, he required them to obey it perfectly to be considered righteous under the law. Breaking any part of the law, was, in effect, breaking the entire law (James 2:10). One strike, and you are "out" forever, so to speak.

- As Paul wrote to the Christians in Rome, the law was not given to humankind to save us. It was given to make us conscious of our sin (Romans 3:20).
- A person is justified by faith apart from the works of the law (Romans 3:28).
- The author of Hebrews recorded a comparison of the old covenant (the law), the new covenant (grace), and our eternal High Priest, Jesus Christ (Hebrews 8:1–2, 6–7).

Why would Christians assume salvation is based on works? What driving force motivates this behavior? One reason may be that human logic says we should be able to prove we are saved. Humans sin. When we were lost, we didn't care. As Christians, hopefully, we care very much. However, try as we may, sin remains a part of our lives even after we accept Jesus Christ as Lord and Savior. Sometimes these sins create doubt and cause troubling questions. Is God willing to save me since I was such a horribly flawed person before I gave my life to Jesus Christ? Is God willing to save me even though I continue to sin after giving my life to Jesus? When God created us, he understood if humanity was given the ability to have faith, they would also have the capacity for doubt. We have been given a living example of this paradox.

> A man brought his demon-possessed son to Jesus's disciples and asked them to drive out the spirit, but they could not. The man told Jesus, "But if you can do anything . . . help us."
>
> "'If you can'?" Jesus said. "Everything is possible for one who believes."
>
> The boy's father exclaimed, "I do believe; help me overcome my unbelief!" (Mark 9:22–24)

Our frail minds can vacillate between faith and doubt, sometimes almost simultaneously. Satan is willing and able, at every opportunity, to help perpetuate doubts in our minds. This result is an ongoing need for proof of God's Holy Spirit living in us. Following this logic, one of the best observable evidences of our genuine faith is good works. They are a natural outcome produced by our internal change (a heart submitted to Jesus and the indwelling Spirit). Jesus told his disciples, "No good tree bears bad fruit, nor does a bad tree bear good fruit.. . . . A good man brings good things out of the good stored up in his heart, and an evil man brings evil things out of the evil stored up in his heart" (Luke 6:43–45).

Deeply flawed human logic creates this problem in the first place. I am often inclined to think everything is about me, that this point of view regarding salvation is about me, but it's not about me. God's plan of salvation is all about him, his love, and what he did for me. Can I do enough, by myself, to deserve to be saved? No! Can I do enough after I have been saved, by myself, to deserve heaven? No! God forgave my sins, past, present, and future, because I am covered by the blood of Jesus's sacrifice, an act that he caused to be completed.

I had the privilege of facilitating a Sunday school class for several years. On numerous occasions we discussed grace versus works in God's plan of salvation. I would end up saying, "For those of you who want a checklist for salvation, here it is. There's only one question: are you indwelt by the Holy Spirit of God? If the answer to the question is 'yes,' then check the box. Otherwise, leave the box blank. If you check the box, you are saved. If you don't check the box, you are not saved." My "checkbox" theory was not the most well-received theory I ever proposed.

We, as flawed humans, can incorrectly apply these verses regarding good works. The worst possible application, as stated earlier, is attempting to apply good works to attaining salvation. Such a plan removes us from grace and places us back under the law. Anyone who relies on the yardstick of works for their salvation may naturally, and erroneously, conclude their sins are not as bad as other people's sins. Such a person may rationalize by thinking something like, "I may have sinned, but at least I didn't commit murder. Moses murdered and he gets to go to heaven." Or, "My sins are certainly less than . . . (fill in the name of the person)." This line of thinking is problematic. For starters, sin is sin in God's eyes. If you break one part of the law you break the entire law. Paul illustrates this when he speaks of wickedness by including those who envy and gossip with murderers and God-haters (Romans 1:29–30). Jesus makes this same point when he, speaking of evils, includes envy and arrogance with murder (Mark 7:20–23).

Another problem with this line of thinking is those who demand a "yardstick" to measure their success are allowed only one human comparison: themselves compared to Jesus Christ. And he never sinned. Grading on a curve or utilizing a sliding scale doesn't apply because Jesus scores 100 percent, perfect in the flesh, regarding sin. How do we measure up? I think David gave the answer for all humans when he said, "My sins have overtaken me . . . They are more than the hairs of my head" (Psalm 40:12). Paul concurred when he wrote, "There is no one righteous, not even one" (Romans 3:10).

The law, the old covenant, required perfection of humankind regarding works. Jesus Christ was the only human (I know, he was fully God as well) who has ever lived or will ever live who met such a high standard. So, God replaced the law with a new covenant of grace because Jesus has become the guarantor of the better covenant. Thanks be to God Almighty. His plan of grace saved us from the law and allowed us to obtain salvation. God's definition of grace, his gift to us that saves us by faith in Jesus Christ, specifically excludes good works. The necessary work for our salvation was completed by one man, Jesus Christ, some two thousand years ago when he hung on a cross in our place for our sins. Our response to his completed work is binary. We either accept or reject God's gift of grace. Since we cannot earn, buy, beg, borrow, or steal God's salvation, our works have no part in gaining our salvation, and we can take no credit for it.

What makes all the difference, under grace, is our love for God the Father, who fashioned the plan to redeem us, and for his Son, Jesus, through whom God's objective was accomplished when Jesus died to pay the debt for our sins. It is about our relationship with God and Jesus. Some may say, "How do I know if I am indwelt by the Holy Spirit? I could trick myself regarding these internal feelings." Such people need more concrete evidence. So, for those who are saved and still want a more tangible checklist, here it is. There's only one question and one checkbox. Do you love God the Father and his Son, Jesus Christ, with all your heart, soul, mind, and strength? If the answer to this question is "yes," then check the box. Otherwise, leave the box blank. If you check the box, you are saved. If you don't check the box, you are not saved.

While our works are of no importance to our salvation, they are of huge importance in our lives after we are saved. "For we are God's handiwork, created in Christ Jesus to do good works, which God prepared in advance for us to do" (Ephesians 2:10). Earlier, I said my single purpose for existing is to bring glory to God in everything I say and do. Because of salvation and the resulting indwelling Holy Spirit, I am able to do good works for God. Before the beginning of time, God Almighty knew exactly when and where each of us would be conceived. He put us in a specific place and time for a reason known to him but unknown to us. To summarize what Paul wrote to the believers at Ephesus, "We are not saved by good works; we are saved for good works."

Jesus confirmed this when he said, "I am the true vine, and my Father is the gardener. He cuts off every branch in me that bears no fruit, while every branch that does bear fruit, he prunes so that it will be even more fruitful. You are already clean because of the word I have spoken to you. Remain in me, as I also remain in you. No branch can bear fruit by itself; it must remain in the vine. Neither can you bear fruit unless you remain in me" (John 15:1–4). God's salvation is a gift to us because of his love for us. Our good works done for the glory of God are simply a by-product, an outflowing of our love for God because he loved us first.

As Christians, we should see an increase of good works bringing glory to the Lord over time. Because we are flawed humans, we will experience inconsistency as we go through seasons with more or less good works. So, do we look at our works, or lack thereof, in a dark season, and conclude we are not saved? No one is going to spend eternity in hell because they lied, stole, hated, murdered, or were gluttonous. People will be separated from God for eternity for one reason only: they did not accept Jesus Christ as their Lord and Savior for the forgiveness of their sins. Conversely, people will be united with God for eternity for one reason only: they did accept Jesus Christ as their Lord and Savior for the forgiveness of their sins. As believers, we are called to love God, Christ, and our fellow people as we follow the leading of the Holy Spirit on our earthly journey.

All Grace and No Wrath—Another Flawed Theology

A cursory perusal of God's Word shows his wrath is mentioned dozens of times. God is jealous and avenging (Nahum 1:2), perfectly so to those who deserve it. He is also a righteous judge who displays his wrath every day (Psalm 7:11). The Bible describes the day of God's wrath, when his righteous judgment will be revealed. Those who are self-seeking and reject the truth will suffer his wrath and anger. Some people say these passages relating to God's wrath speak of some sort of punishment here on earth, up to and including death, but insist there will be no eternal punishment or torment. However, Jesus was very specific regarding eternal life and eternal punishment. "Then he will say to those on his left, 'Depart from me, you who are cursed, into the eternal fire prepared for the devil and his angels . . . Then they will go away to eternal punishment, but the righteous to eternal life" (Matthew 25:41, 46).

Scripture describes, in simple language, the two eternal choices facing every human. Either we accept Jesus Christ as Lord and Savior and spend eternity with him in his kingdom, or we reject Jesus and spend eternity in torment with Satan and his demons. From a human perspective, it is appealing to think heaven exists, but hell does not. Then we could have the good without the bad. Is it possible for heaven to exist but hell not to exist? Scripture tells us both heaven and hell exist eternally. Still, some people claim there must be some other plausible explanation. They believe an all-loving God would never allow people to suffer torment in hell for eternity. Following this logic, they conclude in such a circumstance, God would not be an all-loving God. I will agree with the proponents of this theory—to this extent only. Our God, who is all-loving, would no more allow a person to suffer torment for eternity in hell for rejecting Jesus as Lord and Savior than he would allow his one and only Son to be falsely accused, beaten beyond recognition, and then murdered on a cross by the humans he came to save. Therefore, if you don't believe in the one, how can you believe in the other? Besides, humans cannot possibly fathom the mind of God. Only the Spirit of God can understand his mind.

One final thought on the uniqueness of Scripture. I understand God's thoughts are infinitely higher than our thoughts. Therefore, the most intelligent human, who truly loves the Lord and studies the Bible for a lifetime, will only glean relatively few of the pearls of wisdom contained therein. I also understand God conveyed his plan of salvation through Jesus Christ and how we should live for him in a way a twelve-year-old could understand. But if our foundation is not built on the rock of God's Word, how can we be sure we are going to heaven? How can we be sure we are correctly pointing others to an eternal home with Jesus? We need to ask God Almighty to teach us the true meaning of his Word through the Holy Spirit, so we can live squarely within his will without doubt.

Chapter 7

The Struggle with Servanthood

> Then Jesus said to his disciples, "Whoever wants to be my disciple must deny themselves and take up their cross and follow me. For whoever wants to save their life will lose it, but whoever loses their life for me will find it. (Matthew 16:24–25)

Believing God's Word is one thing. Committing myself to applying it wholeheartedly to my life is another matter entirely. Abdicating the throne of self can be a daunting task. The application involves not only denying myself by setting aside my self-centered desires but doing so for the express purpose of serving others. In my human nature, I don't want to serve but be served. I don't simply want to be "king of my castle;" I want to be the "king of my life." Counteracting this urge requires perpetual perseverance as I labor to achieve God's purpose for my life. Consequently, another time when I am great at self-delusion is when I am trying to convince myself it is OK if I don't do something I know God wants me to do—to do something else, nothing at all, or what I would rather do. The number of excuses I can invent in these circumstances is limited only by my imagination. The following are a few of the more common fallacies I have either employed myself or heard expressed by other Christians.

I'm a Failure
(Which Could Mean Let Someone Else Do It)

Just because we have confessed and repented of our sins does not mean our sins end. After this one-time event, it will still take the rest of our lives for us to be transformed to look more like Christ. This metamorphosis will not be complete until the Lord returns, and we go into eternity with him. All Christians want their sins to decrease over time, but as long as we live in these temporary bodies, sin will be present. Some people may fail regularly because of a struggle with a particular sin. As a result of the human propensity to engage in repetitive sin, some people may claim they are a failure and, therefore, do not deserve to serve the Lord. This is a dangerous position to take. Why would anyone accept Jesus Christ as Lord and Savior, believing their unavoidable subsequent sin would exclude them from God's kingdom? Or why would anyone believe they are saved yet not be good enough to witness to the world? Christians cannot wait until their witness is perfect to act, since they will never reach perfection here on earth. So, we admit our human failures as we witness. Besides, everyone knows humans aren't perfect.

If we claim we are not good enough to witness, what are we saying about the power of the blood of Jesus Christ? Is his sacrifice sufficient to cover every sin, past, present, and future? I hope every believer's answer is "yes." If the answer is "no," then we are all doomed, still living under the law without hope. Satan would certainly love the opportunity to convince us we are failures and should stop all efforts to live for the Lord. However, those who love the Lord know that even when we are unfaithful to him, he remains faithful to us. At times our failures may impair or negate our Christian witness to one or more persons. In such times, God will use others to point the way to the kingdom of heaven while we are being restored. Hopefully, such instances will be the exception rather than the rule in our lives.

While our family lived in Dayton, Ohio, one of my sons and my daughter gave their lives to Jesus Christ as their Lord and Savior. Susie and I still had one unsaved child in our household. If anyone had said I would live in Louisville one day I would have told them they were crazy. While working in Dayton I had reached the highest level I could attain there. On occasion, Susie and I would talk about what I might do next regarding my career. Eventually I applied for a management position and, in 1999, our family moved to Louisville.

Prior to leaving Dayton, I identified some Christian churches in the Louisville area. There seemed to be quite a few choices. Fern Creek Christian Church was on our short list of places to visit. The first time I set foot in their building was on a Wednesday evening in May 1999. I could feel the Holy Spirit moving there. As spiritually obtuse as I can be sometimes, I knew the palpable presence of the Spirit couldn't be manufactured. I also knew if that wasn't the place where the Lord wanted me, I couldn't wait to see where he did want me to be. Coincidence? I don't think so. It was a God-incidence. This body of believers became hugely important to my family.

The transition to life in Kentucky was not going well for our unsaved son. He wasn't integrating at school or church, and our disagreements grew. I was concerned for his salvation. Yet, in my anger, I was losing my witness with him. We talked less and less. So, Susie, beginning with two of her friends, Kari and Ann, started recruiting prayer warriors in earnest. It still didn't seem to be enough. Susie recruited Steve, the youth minister, to see if he might be a stabilizing male influence in our son's life. In October 2002 I had an argument with my son, and he left home. The prayer warriors increased the intensity of their petitions. Susie was convinced the Lord was convicting our son.

November 20, 2002, was my dad's seventy-fifth birthday. By then I believed my son was never coming home. What I had given up as lost, Susie had given over to the Lord—and he was listening. God used a special tool to prick our son's heart. My dad had been praying that the Lord would give him the right words when—not if but when—the opportunity presented itself. Shortly after calling my dad to wish him a happy birthday, our broken-hearted son called and then returned home. However, coming home was only the first step. The critical step still lay ahead as God's Spirit had our son squarely in his sights. The prayer warriors increased the intensity of their prayers. These Christians knew the power of their prayers and were waiting expectantly to see the hand of God move in our son's life. God loves intercessors; just as Jesus Christ interceded for all humanity. God waits for the opportunity to respond to prayers made in his will by those who love him.

The day after our son returned home, shortly before Thanksgiving, Susie and I left for West Virginia to be with my dad, who was going to take a stress test at his cardiologist's office. My plan was to go to West Virginia to drive Dad to the doctor's office, return home to get the family, and then go back to West Virginia to celebrate Thanksgiving. Little did I know God had other plans.

Dad's stress test was stopped in progress, and he was sent by ambulance from the doctor's office to the hospital emergency room. Dad needed quadruple bypass open-heart surgery as soon as possible. I knew I wasn't going home to bring anyone back to West Virginia. God had a better idea anyway. He was arranging transportation to bring our son to West Virginia. So, six days after returning home, our son was on his way to see his Papa before surgery. My buddy, Rick, bad back and all, drove five hundred miles round trip, so he would have time on the road to witness to a "captive audience." As a result of Dad's surgery, our son had the opportunity to see how a Christian, his grandfather, could face life-threatening circumstances without fear.

As the surgeons repaired dad's heart, the greatest physician operated on our son's heart. On Sunday, December 1, 2002, our son was baptized into the Lord Jesus Christ. As a Christian husband and father, seeing my entire family covered by the blood of Jesus was my greatest desire. The last part of that desire was achieved through the help of my brothers and sisters in Christ when our son was baptized. Just as Moses stood in the breach many times between life and death for the Israelites, my fellow believers stood in the breach repeatedly for my son. God used many people including Susie, Rick, Ann, Kari, Steve, and several others, to stand in the gap for our child. I failed utterly in my witness to my son during a critical time because our relationship was virtually nonexistent. However, the Body of Christ came together and petitioned the Holy Spirit to work as only he can.

When we fail due to sin, guilt is a common result. Here are several important points to remember regarding guilt.

- It's a double-edged sword; it can be both good and bad.
- It's a fact of life for almost all humans.
- Two powerful forces are at work before and after sin takes place: the Spirit of God and Satan.

When we sin, we will either experience remorse or not. If we experience no remorse after we sin, it could be an indication of a hardening heart or, even worse, a seared conscience, which is perilous spiritual ground. Most of us, if not all who claim to love Jesus, feel remorse after sin. The question becomes, is this a worldly sorrow (because we got caught for what we did) or a godly sorrow (because we failed God and truly desire to obey him)? As Scripture says, "Godly sorrow brings repentance that leads to salvation and leaves no regret, but worldly sorrow brings death (2 Corinthians 7:10). When we sin against God, he wants us to be truly sorry for what we have done, repent of our sin, and try harder to live for him, as we have been instructed. On the other hand, Satan's desire is for our sin to paralyze us and drive us further away from God. He wants us to wallow in our sinfulness, respond with self-pity, and turn away from our Father in heaven. Here's the tricky part: it is a good thing to feel guilty for our sin. It is proof our consciences have not been seared. When this guilt leads to godly sorrow and repentance, we are restored to a right relationship with God. However, if we repent and then allow the guilt of the sin to paralyze us; keeping us from doing the good works God has called us to complete, we are sinning again. Therefore, the guilt is bad. How we deal with the guilt is what matters.

Saul, a Pharisee from Tarsus who later became known as Paul, is one example of a flawed human who met Jesus Christ, fell in love with him, and was used mightily by God to further the kingdom of heaven. Paul reminds us clearly of the daily struggle he faced in his war with sin, even after his conversion. He openly admitted that he did not do the things he wanted to do, and the things he hated to do, he did. Do you think there may have been days when Paul felt like he was losing the battle? No matter how he felt, Paul never gave up. He was laser focused on his mission. Regardless of his personal struggles with sin, he refused to be distracted. Paul never stopped preaching the Lord Jesus Christ crucified, buried, and resurrected. How is your battle with sin going these days? Are you dealing with different sins, or is one repetitive sin haunting you? Maybe you have reached a point in your walk with the Lord where sin is an occasional or even rare occurrence. You can be sure of one thing regarding your struggle with sin: you are not alone! Stay focused on the most important matter!

Scripture provides us with a well-known lineup of saints from the ancient days who loved the Lord and remained faithful to the end. I remember hearing, and later reading, about these people and the heroic acts they performed through the power of God. As I have studied these people in depth, I find we are more alike than I first thought. Like the Old Testament saints, Christians today love the Lord even though we fail repeatedly in our walk with God. Consider the following facts.

- At a time when God's heart was filled with pain at people's evil inclinations, he chose Noah to continue the human race. Noah was one

of only eight people (he and his family) who survived the great flood. Yet, after the flood, Noah planted a vineyard, got drunk, and lay naked in his tent (Genesis 9:20–21).
- Abram was chosen to be a father of nations when the Lord called him to leave his native land. Yet, not once but twice he willingly gave Sarai, his wife, to be another man's wife to protect himself (Genesis 12:11–15; 20:1–2).
- God chose Moses to lead his people to the Promised Land. As a young man, Moses murdered an Egyptian for beating a Hebrew slave (Exodus 2:11–12).
- The Lord was prepared to kill Moses, who had not circumcised his son, but Moses's wife, Zipporah, saved his life by doing what Moses should have done (Exodus 4:24–26).
- David, a man after God's own heart, was chosen to lead the Israelite people, yet David was an adulterer and a murderer (2 Samuel 11:4, 14-15).

Pointing out the shortcomings of these people is not an attempt to judge or belittle them but rather to show how God uses people who love him for his good purposes. Scripture tells us that God "chose the foolish things of the world to shame the wise; the weak things of the world to shame the strong; and the lowly things of this world to nullify the things that are; so that no one may boast before him (1 Corinthians 1:27–29) and that in our weaknesses, he makes us strong (2 Corinthians 12:10).

Noah, Abram, Moses, and David are just a few examples of people who loved God but who struggled in their walk with the Lord because of their sins. God did not condemn these people because of their failures. He forgave them, lifting them up for their faith in him and their love for him, and used them to show his awesome power. Isn't it inspiring to know these flawed, sinful people were commended for their faith? We should feel encouraged knowing God was not ashamed to be called their God. One final point on this matter: humans cannot eliminate failure. It is inevitable for us. It also provides a vital, positive benefit to believers by keeping us humble. It is reassuring for me to know these "heroes of the faith" were far from perfect, but they still received the crown of life. That means we can too.

Let's return for a moment to the story of Paul, who, prior to his conversion, was known as Saul of Tarsus. Saul was a Jew who was trained in the law by a renowned teacher. He was a rising star in Judaism at a young age. Saul was zealous for God, persecuting Christians by having them imprisoned or killed. I try to understand what it was like for him the day he met Jesus on the road to Damascus. In my mind, I go back and place myself in Saul's shoes. I'm a young man on a fast track to prominence in the Jewish faith, and I have just been sent out on a holy mission. I am fully convinced by stamping out this heretical cult made up of people called Christians, I am fulfilling my duty to God in good conscience. As I march down a dusty road with letters of condemnation in my pocket, I am formalizing my plan to accomplish the arrest of some of these heathens when I reach Damascus.

Suddenly, I am struck by a thunderbolt of blazing light. As the cobwebs start to clear in my head, I find myself lying face down in the road. My initial disorientation quickly gives way to fear. What just happened? I cannot see anything. Then I hear a voice. Jesus is accusing me of persecuting him. I ask myself, "How can this be?" I have dedicated my life to the Lord's work. The truth settles into my mind as quickly as the flash of light came. The Lord, the Holy One, has accused me. The accusation is perfectly true, and I am defenseless. I feel sick to my stomach, and it's not just because I swallowed some dust from the road as I fell. The guilt and shame are oppressive. The full weight of my actions as a persecutor of Christians lies heavy on my heart. The "good work" I thought I was doing for God was all wrong. What am I going to do?

Back to the present. What would I do if I were lying face down on a dusty road while being confronted by my Lord? I can only hope I would make the same choice Saul made. The choice he made had profound consequences on the rest of his life. It is exceedingly difficult to reject the "truths" on which your entire life has been based. If faced with such a dilemma, I think many people might simply give up. Not Saul. Knowing the source of this revelation, Saul rejected the old, errant "truth" he had been taught. Then he embraced the truth, willingly giving his life to his new work in his Lord Jesus Christ. In making that decision, Saul, now Paul, knew he, the persecutor, would become the persecuted. You know the rest of the story.

Have you ever considered yourself a failure, spiritually speaking? I can recall numerous times. A few are outlined in these pages. Let me talk for a moment about myself, not you. The statement "I am a failure" is perfectly true. In my own strength, in my sinful nature, I am destined to fail God Almighty no matter how hard I try to do otherwise. On my own strength, I deserve eternal separation from God. These are irrefutable truths for me.

However, my sins, my failures, do not exclude me from God's family, nor do they disqualify me from engaging in the Lord's work. Quite the contrary, I, like Paul (this is the only way I will compare myself with such a great witness for Christ) admit my sins and imperfections, so others who are imperfect may be encouraged to seek and find Jesus Christ as well. In fact, the only way my sins disqualify me as a witness for Christ is if I am unwilling to admit and repent of them. Thanks be to God Almighty! His plan to redeem me does not rely on my frail, human power or my sinful nature but on his limitless power and merciful grace. Just as God used Saul for the work of the kingdom of heaven, he can use us for the same purpose if we are willing. As frail as humans are, those who are indwelt by the Holy Spirit and diligently follow his leading will never fail.

It's Too Late
(Which Could Mean I Don't Want to Do It)

Scripture gives us numerous examples of humans well advanced in years who were called to the Lord's work.

- Abram was seventy-five years old when God called him to leave his country for an unknown destination.
- Moses was eighty years old when the Lord called him to lead the Israelites out of Egypt.
- Caleb was eighty-five years old when he received the hill country of Hebron as an inheritance in Canaan and attacked the people living there.
- God's promise of a son to Abraham was fulfilled when Abraham was one hundred years old.
- Noah was six hundred years old when he finished building the ark.

People in the earliest days of human civilization lived much longer than we do today, but none of these men were young, even by the lifespan in their day, when the Lord called them. God, who never changes, continues to operate today as he did thousands of years ago. He calls both the young and the elderly to his work. Consider two modern examples of people advanced in years who were called to a specific new ministry.

In December 2018, a Circle of Hope article, "Saints and Holy Days We Want to Remember," highlighted Clara McBride Hale, stating that,

> Clara Hale had a mission of motherhood. Her life experiences helped make her extraordinarily empathetic to the pain and suffering of other mothers and children . . . Clara's husband lost his battle with cancer when Clara was 27. Clara retired in 1968 at age 63 and . . . started Hale's House in 1969 when . . . her daughter . . . brought a mother and child who were addicted to drugs to Hale's home . . . Mother Hale, as she became known . . . eventually helped over 2,000 drug addicted babies and young children who were born addicted to drugs . . . On February 6, 1985, at the close of the State of the Union message to Congress, President Ronald Reagan . . . recognized "Mother Hale" for helping babies of drug–addicted mothers in Harlem.[1]

The history page of Child Evangelism Fellowship's website provides a brief biography of the organization's founder.

> In 1937, Jesse Irvin Overholtzer founded Child Fellowship, a Bible-centered, worldwide organization whose purpose was to evangelize boys and girls with the gospel of the Lord Jesus Christ . . . Jesse at the age of 12 was convicted of his own sin and sought counsel from his mother. He was told, "Son, you are too young." It wasn't until Overholtzer was in college that he heard the gospel and trusted Christ as his Savior. Later, as a pastor, Mr. Overholtzer read one of Charles Spurgeon's sermons that stated, "A child of five, if properly instructed can as truly believe and be regenerated as an adult." The Lord used this statement in Mr. O's life to lead him to begin the ministry of Child Evangelism Fellowship when he was 60 years old. The ministry has grown into the largest evangelistic outreach to children in the world, with over 2,900 missionaries overseas and approximately 40,000 volun-

teers. Child Evangelism Fellowship is currently ministering in countries around the world and in every state in the U.S.[2]

Clara and Jesse could have been retired, enjoying their golden years in leisure after working their entire lives, but they didn't allow age or anything else to become a hindrance when the Holy Spirit called them to a specific ministry.

On occasion I have heard Christians comment about retiring from the Lord's work, though they don't actually use the word retire. If you've been part of a Christian congregation for long, you've heard requests from ministers and elders calling for volunteers to help staff various ministries. Every children's ministry I have ever known has consistently needed additional help. When the necessary number of volunteers don't step forward, the leadership may attempt to recruit people individually. Sometimes the response from an elderly Christian goes something like, "I've served for years. It's time for someone else to take a turn."

Each believer will make his or her own decision regarding whether to continue participating in a particular ministry within the Body of Christ and how much time they will devote to such an endeavor. Circumstances can restrict the amount of time a person has available to volunteer. As we get older, our energy levels tend to decrease, further impacting our engagement in ministry. However, the Lord is always calling us to contribute in some fashion to furthering the kingdom of heaven.

Prior to Adam and Eve sinning, I think life in the Garden of Eden was as perfect as life gets on this earth. They didn't have to work by the sweat of their brows for food. God provided it; it was theirs for the taking. Since sin and death had not entered the world, there was no sickness or disease. It was paradise. Yet, even in this idyllic setting, Adam and Eve couldn't spend all day engaging in leisurely pursuits. God had chores for them to do. However, these assignments in the Garden of Eden were joyous and delightful, not burdensome toil. Adam was to take care of the garden and name all the birds and animals. I believe Eden was a pale, earthly foreshadowing of our future eternal home. One day believers will praise and serve God in heaven, though the specifics of this service are not identified. I have a friend who has been known to say, "If we think we're going to spend eternity sitting on a cloud playing a harp, we have the wrong picture of heaven."

As I understand the parable of the workers in the vineyard (Matthew 20:1), God is the landowner, the workers are believers, the vineyard is the earth, and the day is the lifetime of the workers. God called different people, some very early in their life (first thing in the morning), some later in life (third, sixth, and ninth hours), and some very late in life (the eleventh hour) to his work. Those who were hired very late in life (the eleventh hour) received the same reward (eternal life with God) as those who had worked all day (their entire lives). Also, those hired at the eleventh hour were expected to labor for the one hour left in the day. God didn't release any of the workers before the end of the day no matter what hour he called them.

I have found only one passage in Scripture regarding retirement. The Lord told Moses that the Levites working at the tent of meeting must retire from their regular service at the age of fifty and work no longer. However, the Lord did not release these men from continuing to serve Him but changed their role from providing labor to providing counsel and assistance. The Lord told Moses, "They may assist their brothers in performing their duties at the tent of meeting, but they themselves must not do the work (Numbers 8:23–26). Elderly Christians should not have to do the "heavy lifting" in ministry. Let the young folks with strong backs and seemingly endless energy take care of those duties. But the elderly should always be participating by sharing with the younger folks their precious gifts of godly wisdom and decades of experience in Christian living.

> Jesus told the crowd, "Do not work for food that spoils, but for food that endures to eternal life."
>
> Then the crowd asked Jesus, "What must we do to do the works God requires?'
>
> Jesus answered, "The work of God is this: to believe in the one he has sent." (John 6:27–29)

We are never called to "retire" from belief in Jesus Christ. Belief requires action. If we are breathing, God has a ministry with some type of work for each of us to complete.

There's Always Tomorrow (Which Could Mean I'd Rather be Doing Something Else Right Now)

When I was stationed at the US naval base in Sicily, almost everything was different from what I had experienced before. Sicilians didn't just talk and look different; they lived differently. Life in Sicily was slow and easy. Businesses and shops, except for the larger cities, would shut down for several hours in the afternoon for lunchtime and rest at home. These businesses would reopen in the late afternoon until early evening. I lived in a small town in the foothills of Mount Etna, an active volcano on the island. One paved road led from the town where I lived to the base where I worked. It had numerous potholes. Every so often a worker would bring a load of dirt mixed with rock and fill the holes in the asphalt, but after a few rain showers and more traffic, the holes would be empty again and grow larger. Every once in a great while, a crew would pack the potholes with asphalt, tamping the patch with a hand tool. Temporary fixes didn't come often, but they were far more numerous than permanent fixes. It seemed to me the philosophy of life in Sicily was "don't do today what you can put off until tomorrow."

Time is the second most precious gift afforded us by our Maker, surpassed only by the grace he extends to us. After all, without God's grace, life would have no eternal meaning. In the grand scheme of world history, the span of a human life is very short. The number of days of our lives are known to God but not to us. At most they are fleeting, like an evening shadow, a mist, or a breath. This is an obvious fact some of us would rather ignore since we aren't overly fond of pondering our mortality. However, it is not only humans whose lifespan is short. The existence of our planet is also finite, temporary. Just as the human body wears out with injury, illness, and age, our world is also decaying, passing away from the disease of sin. Paul explained this to the body of believers at Corinth two thousand years ago when he told them to focus on undivided devotion to the Lord since time is short because this world in its present form is passing away (1 Corinthians 7:29–31). Both the world and us are getting older. Furthermore, we are living in the "last days." Scripture says ". . . in these last days he (God) has spoken to us by his Son." (Hebrews 1:1–2). For these reasons and others, time becomes more precious to me as I get older.

In the past I took the gift of time for granted by counting on tomorrow. When I look back on my life and think of the opportunities squandered, I admit my procrastination was an obscene extravagance. I recall several occasions in my adult life while I was lost in my sins when I could have (and should have) died. However, God, in his infinite mercy, spared me. As the adage goes, "There's always tomorrow," but we know this statement simply isn't true. It would be far more accurate for us to say we expect tomorrow to occur. We can even rationalize by hypothesizing the odds are greatly in our favor that we will be here tomorrow, but we have no guarantee. Death comes to us all, and most of us don't know when it will happen.

I tend to identify with people who draw the same conclusions I do or admit to the same mistakes I've made. I find some reassurance knowing I am not alone in my failures (there goes my warped human logic at work again). In his book, *Tender Warrior*, Stu Weber talks about several wake-up calls he received, saying, "I knew that I had been living by a 'second chance philosophy of life.' I had always figured . . . there's always tomorrow."[3] Such a philosophy also conveys an alternative message: there is no urgency today. Nothing could be further from the truth. Even if we are here tomorrow, it is possible the person to whom we are to witness will not be. Paul understood the urgency when he told the believers in Corinth, "I tell you, now is the time of God's favor, now is the day of salvation" (2 Corinthians 6:2).

I was planning to take my family to Mom and Dad's house for the fourth of July weekend in 1996. Little did I know I was going to make the trip not for the reason I planned. In the early morning hours of Tuesday, July 2, I received a call from my younger brother, Timmy, telling me his twin brother, Jimmy, was dead. Instead of going to celebrate a major holiday with my family, I went to grieve with them. When Jimmy died, I had been a Christian for over three years, but I had done precious little to witness to my brother. I knew my family would witness to him. What a dangerous attitude, particularly when dealing with eternal matters. For Jimmy, on July 2, 1996, tomorrow would never come.

I never heard Jimmy express faith in Jesus Christ as his Lord and Savior. I don't know where he will spend eternity. I can only hope he made things right with the Lord before he died.

After Jimmy's funeral, I was thinking about him one day when I recalled a specific event involving both of us. Jimmy and I walked out of Mom and Dad's house after a rain. There was a vivid, beautiful rainbow in the sky. Jimmy asked why there were rainbows. Though he didn't say it, I knew he didn't want to know about differing refractions of light through droplets of water in the sky producing multiple colors. I told him how God, after flooding the entire world, promised Noah he would never destroy the earth by water again and then placed a rainbow in the sky after it rained as a sign of the promise he had made to Noah. We stood there silently as Jimmy stared at the rainbow for quite some time. Then Jimmy started walking again, and we went about doing whatever it was we went outside to do. This is a bittersweet memory for me. The sweet part is, it was a brief, straightforward conversation between the two of us as Jimmy pondered God. The bitter part is, it's the only conversation I can recall having with Jimmy about the Lord.

One day Jesus may ask me why I didn't introduce Jimmy to him, why I didn't have a sense of urgency to point my younger brother to the kingdom of heaven. I can truthfully say Mom, Dad, and Timmy witnessed to Jimmy whenever the opportunity arose, but any response I offer will be exceedingly lame at best. As an adult I didn't have a good relationship with Jimmy. Consequently, we didn't talk about much of anything of import. I was at least as responsible as Jimmy for our poor relationship. As a Christian and an older brother, I should have done everything possible to make things right, but I was living out of state (another lame excuse), and I didn't make any effort. This was another of my greater failings (by my own estimation) as a believer. Jimmy's death provided me with one of the most expensive lessons I have ever learned. When it comes to spiritual matters, I don't have the luxury of waiting. I must seize every opportunity the Lord presents to me.

What is the underlying motivation driving some Christians to procrastinate? Several reasons come to mind. People could be lazy, or the task to be completed may be difficult or unpleasant. As Christians, we should be excited about working for the kingdom of heaven and diligently seek to recognize the opportunities the Lord places in our path. Certainly, the Body of Christ is not exempt from laziness. Such people will procrastinate regarding everything they do except those few things most pleasurable to, or profitable for, them. This condition is easy to realize, over time, for those who know such a person. Rarely will lazy people tell you they won't do something. They simply don't act. As time passes, it becomes apparent they don't intend to act. If asked about the progress, or lack thereof, they will make up any number of excuses, but this inaction conveys a clear message: "I don't want to do it now. I may not ever want to do it."

God may be calling you to engage another Christian in a very difficult conversation, one that may produce hurt feelings. To make matters worse, you may detest confrontation. Few people get excited about starting or completing such a task, but no matter what excuse I offer for inaction regarding the kingdom of heaven, it is only to give me a reason for not doing what I don't want to do. I don't want to admit that I don't want to do it. If placed in a position where I must give a definitive reason for my procrastination, my best excuse is "I can't." In the sinful, human sense, this statement is perfectly true. I cannot do anything good or walk as Christ walked on my own. But I am not on my own. When a Christian says, "I can't," what is the person saying about the power of the indwelling Holy Spirit? The twenty-first century is not the first time a human has questioned God's power. God asked his people through the prophet Isaiah, "Was my arm too short to deliver you? Do I lack the strength to rescue you?" (Isaiah 50:2).

By the power of the Spirit of God, the universe was created, and Jesus Christ was raised from the dead. So, is his power sufficient to enable each of us to complete the tasks he has assigned to us? I hope the answer of every Christian is "Yes." We can accomplish anything through his power if it is in his will. Every day, I need to make the most of my short time walking this earth, diligently seeking the opportunities the Holy Spirit places before me to make a positive impact for the kingdom of heaven.

The Hindering Truth—I Don't Want to Be Peculiar

Earlier, I discussed some basic human motivators, including: desiring relationships with others, loving and being loved, being valued by others, and being considered significant by ourselves and others. As I look at these fundamental needs, it is easy to see why believers, from both a human and a spiritual perspective, would be motivated to do good works. My own personal experience indicates Christians do a pretty good job at helping those in need and in building up the Body of Christ. However, I don't necessarily see the same enthusiasm for reaching the lost with the message of Jesus Christ.

Fear of rejection or ridicule is a predominant reason why Christians procrastinate or fail to act in the Lord's work, particularly when it regards witnessing to the unsaved. Even though we live in this world, we are not to be of this world (John 17:14) because we belong to Jesus Christ. However, many Christians, don't want to be viewed as different from the world because of the resulting consequences. Many times, those who are different from others around them are ridiculed and rejected. I have no desire to be treated that way. It's embarrassing, hurtful, and damaging to my psyche. This problem has plagued Christians since Jesus walked the earth. Scripture tells us many believed in Jesus but "would not openly acknowledge their faith for fear they would be put out of the synagogue for they loved human praise more than praise from God" (John 12:42–43).

One defining characteristic of those who love the Lord should include being "peculiar," different. From the time God chose the Israelites through to the present, he has always desired his people to be distinct, set apart from the rest of the world (Leviticus 20:23–26). Some of the reasons for this distinction are that God has always wanted his people to willingly choose him as their King, to serve him by obeying his commands, and to serve as a righteous example for the rest of the world. The Israelites wanted to be like the other nations. They wanted an earthly king rather than God as king (I Samuel 8:4–7) because they didn't want to be different. In our sinful nature, we carry this desire to the extreme. We want no king at all other than ourselves because the king sets all the rules. As God's Word tells us more than once, "In those days Israel had no king; everyone did as they saw fit" (Judges 17:6).

What we see in our basic needs is a very real human conflict for a Christian. We want to be accepted and valued by both humans and God, but Scripture tells us we won't be accepted or valued. The world is not particularly receptive to "peculiar people" whose faith is opposed to every other faith. Many people say eternity doesn't exist or that all paths lead to heaven. These are only two of many errant theories proposed by non-believers. Christians say the only way to eternal life is through faith in Jesus Christ as Lord and Savior, and the only alternative to salvation is eternity in hell. Jesus warned us, "You will be hated by everyone because of me" (Matthew 10:22). Knowing this, we still hold out hope the world will accept us because we fear being ridiculed, rejected, and ostracized. The unsaved know this. Those who don't want to hear what we have to say know one of their best defenses is to ridicule and reject us. To make matters worse, Christians in America have led a sheltered life when it comes to persecution for their faith compared to believers in many other countries. Such naivete leaves us ill-equipped to deal with significant opposition to our faith.

Our society, in very insidious ways, also promotes an attitude of "significance of self." It's scary knowing the children and grandchildren of today, mine and yours, are being raised in a society that frowns on chastising children for their mistakes lest we damage their self-esteem. Society encourages us to bolster our children's self-esteem by praising everything they do. As mature Christians, we need to encourage our children while also correcting any "self-pampering" we observe in them. We need to help them prepare for the spiritual war they will face for the rest of their lives. Today more than ever, believers in America are facing a growing number of detractors whose hostility against the Christian message is increasing daily.

Pastor and author Brian Jones says in his book, *Hell is Real (But I Hate to Admit It)*, "In my experience as a pastor, plain and simple embarrassment has done more to derail the evangelistic passion of Christ followers than the other three (reasons) combined . . . Embarrassment stems from the need for anyone, not just Christians, to feel accepted and loved by friends and family. In fact, our longing for acceptance is much more powerful than our desire for money, sex, or power."[4] Brian continues, "Acceptance and embarrassment go hand in hand. Lack of one produces the other . . . The problem is that a Christian who believes in hell and believes people who don't accept Jesus will go there for eternity is never going to be accepted by his or her non-Christian friends."[5]

Are we to refrain from presenting the gospel message to a lost friend because he or she might reject us? If a lost person is truly my friend, and I present the message of salvation to that person in a sincere, humble manner, can't that person reject the offer without rejecting my friendship? The fact is, we can speak the truth to the lost without provoking ridicule or hostility. This is one reason for building solid relationships before witnessing. By our words and deeds, we show whether we are seeking the approval of people or God. We run the risk of rejection by people if we speak the truth or risk rejection by God if we remain silent regarding our faith. Paul addressed this choice with the saved souls in Galatia by posing a question and an answer: "Am I now trying to win the approval of human beings, or of God? Or am I trying to please people? If I were still trying to please people, I would not be a servant of Christ" (Galatians 1:10). The message of Christians to the world must be clear and unequivocal regardless of the world's response. Some have credited Saint John Chrysostom with saying, "We must not mind insulting men, if by respecting them we offend God." We must endeavor to insult neither. As always, we must convey the truth correctly and plainly, amply seasoned with humility and love. We are responsible to make our best effort in this regard. The recipients are responsible for their response.

Chapter 8

The Struggle Against Flesh and Blood

"I have told you these things, so that in me you may have peace. In this world you will have trouble. But take heart! I have overcome the world." (John 16:33)

As we attempt to live a Christ-like life utilizing self-assessment as a tool for improvement, we will realize our internal impediments. We always struggle internally with our sinful nature. We also probably struggle on occasion with God's Word and our willingness to submit ourselves to the Lord as his servants. In addition to internal difficulties with living a Christian life, we face external challenges as well. One of these obstacles comes in the form of other people. We must remain vigilant of those around us during these rapidly changing times. Vigilance has nothing to do with fear, hysteria, or paranoia. Quite the opposite, it is deliberate observation whose purpose is to identify and understand potential difficulties in our world. Life is filled with many kinds of trouble. If we are attentive, we may recognize a pattern in our homeland today that was foretold by God thousands of years ago. This knowledge should enable us to determine the best way to maintain our Christian walk while witnessing to others and to realize the golden opportunities that current events present to believers.

Wars and Rumors of Wars

Armed conflicts have been in existence almost as long as humanity has existed. The first battle recorded in Scripture occurred during the time of Abraham (Genesis 14:1–2). Wars have continued around the world ever since. A 2020 report, "American War and Military Operations Casualties: Lists and Statistics," by the Congressional Research Service, lists ten principal wars in which the United States participated from 1775 through to 1991.[1] Five of these, the American Revolution, the War of 1812, the Mexican War, the Civil War, and the Spanish American War, were fought, in whole or in part on American soil. But we don't need these facts to understand we live in a world filled with war. Rarely does a week pass without an armed conflict somewhere around the globe being highlighted in the news. Such wars used to seem far away to me. Not so much anymore.

Change Is in the Wind

Growing up during the 1950s and the early 1960s was, for me, a time of carefree pleasure. As an adult looking through family photo albums, I came across pictures of two events I remember like they were yesterday. One picture is of me sitting outside Aunt Ruth's house on a bright summer day. My head is propped on the knee of my cousin, Robert, and I'm asleep. The other shows Larry and Suzy, two of my cousins, with me at the swimming pool in Madison, West Virginia. Fun, food, and rest when absolutely required were the only concerns in my life back then.

When I was almost six years old, Mom had twin sons who were energetic and impish. You can imagine the time and energy required to care for these two youngsters, whom she lovingly nicknamed "Heckle and Jeckle." (For those who may be too young to remember, Heckle and Jeckle were cartoon characters when I was a kid, two magpies who were always getting into mischief). With Mom focused entirely on my two younger brothers, I was a free man. Not only was my time my own, I didn't have any of the worries of today's world. My greatest worries back then were who I would play with that day, being home for lunch, and being home for supper. I grew up in a time and a place where we didn't worry about children being kidnapped. I could go play cops and robbers with the neighborhood friends in the morning if I was home in time for lunch. Then, in the afternoon, it might be a game of hide-and-seek. It was important to be home in time for supper since we ate as a family. Dad wasn't happy if his mashed potatoes started to get cold because he was waiting for me to come home. As a teenager, the Boys' Club and Boy Scouts were my major activities.

Not only was life fun and carefree, it was, for the most part, uncomplicated because the rules were straightforward. Don't lie. Take responsibility for your actions. We could even look up to our sports superstars, like Jerry West and Brooks Robinson, as decent role models. Kids were expected to obey adults even if they weren't our parents because the adults who lived in our neighborhood wouldn't tell us to do something wrong. Going to church was a popular thing to do, even for non-Christians. We had one car in our family (until I was sixteen years old), and Mom didn't drive. Sunday was reserved for God, good food, and socializing with family and friends. "Those were the good old days," as every generation before me has said. Without a doubt, life was much simpler and slower when I was a child.

During my childhood and teenage years, change was in the wind, ominous changes that even a youngster could understand. Documents contained in the National Archives and Records Administration reveal:

- In August 1963, Martin Luther King Jr. delivered his famous "I Have a Dream" speech to a massive crowd of civil rights marchers gathered in front of the Lincoln Memorial in Washington, DC.[2] His dream lasted only a few years longer.
- In September 1963, the Sixteenth Street Baptist Church in Birmingham, Alabama, was bombed, killing four girls.[3]
- In November 1963, our principal entered our classroom and announced President John Kennedy had been assassinated.[4] It was the first time I can recall seeing adults crying in school.
- In February 1965, Malcolm X was assassinated while addressing a human rights group in New York City.[5]
- In 1968, a trifecta of chaos occurred. Vietnam War protests were raging. Meanwhile, Martin Luther King Jr. and Robert Kennedy were assassinated.[6]

These six tempestuous years ensured I knew the times were changing. What I still didn't understand back then was these changes were long term, if not permanent. What I was experiencing was just the beginning. The forces of hate and chaos were gaining momentum in America like a big rock rolling downhill.

Increasing Chaos

When I was a teenager, I heard and read reports of violence in many different parts of the world. As a young man, I was serving in the US Navy, stationed in Sicily. I flew into Catania, Sicily, on two occasions from 1974 to 1976. Each time I had to change planes in Rome. What I observed there was an eye-opener for me. As I went from one gate to another in the airport, soldiers or police officers there were armed with machine guns. Others were armed with a variety of weapons and dogs. They seemed to be everywhere. It was clear the Italians took airport security very seriously. The stories I had heard and read regarding random violence in Europe took on a whole new meaning. It also made me thankful I could walk through any airport in America with complete freedom. While there were significant incidents of bombings on American soil during the 1970s, those events seemed confined to larger cities and were far away from me and my home.

When I was discharged from the Navy in 1976, Susie and I traveled around Europe before returning home. There was significant civil unrest in Spain and Northern Ireland. So, as a precaution, Susie and I decided not to visit those countries. We thoroughly enjoyed our jaunt around Europe. It was the opportunity of a lifetime for us. I was glad when I returned home, but I had to make some adjustments since changes had taken place in the short time I was outside the United States. An interstate had been built through the middle of my hometown, making significant changes to the surface roads. I made more than a few wrong turns until I learned the new routes I had to take. Life at home had changed in the two short years I was gone.

Over the years I have noticed several disturbing changes taking place. Chaos seems to be increasing everywhere in America. The social fabric of our country is disintegrating before our eyes. I was fortunate to have two parents who were married to each other for their entire lives. Mom and Dad had been married sixty-four years when Mom died. Dad died a widower less than three years later. However, lengthy marriages are becoming a relic of days gone by. Consider some of the trends we are witnessing in our homeland today. In

December 2015, the Pew Research Center published an article, "Parenting in America," noting:

> Two-parent households are on the decline in the United States as divorce, remarriage, and cohabitation are on the rise . . .
>
> In the early 1960s babies typically arrived within a marriage. Today . . . four-in-ten births occur to women who . . . are single or living with a non-marital partner . . .

Parents today are raising their children against a backdrop of increasingly diverse and, for many, constantly evolving family forms . . . In 1960, the height of the post-World War II baby boom . . . 73% of all children were living in a family with two married parents in their first marriage. By 1980, 61% of children were living in this type of family, and today less than half (46%) are.[7]

In America, marriage is no longer defined as God intended. According to Findlaw in the case of Obergefell v. Hodges (2015), the Supreme Court held the Fourteenth Amendment requires a state to license a marriage between two people of the same sex and to recognize a marriage between two people of the same sex when their marriage was lawfully licensed and performed out of state.[8]

In 1973, the sanctity of unborn human life was dealt a harsh blow. According to Findlaw, in a summary of the Roe v. Wade case, the Supreme Court decided the United States Constitution provides a fundamental "right to privacy" that protects a woman's right to choose whether to have an abortion.[9]

More recently we have seen efforts to erode the sanctity of life even further. In 2019 and 2020, legislators and politicians in several states considered or introduced legislation making abortion on demand easier to obtain later in a pregnancy. I have even heard and read about politicians advocating for a deformed infant being left to die after birth. Abortion has been the law of the land in America for almost fifty years. These latest developments are a "natural" next step in our existing laws. So, I ask myself, will I live to see suicide on demand for those who are tired of living? Will I live to see euthanasia of the elderly because they are no longer "productive" members of society or their medical treatment is costing the government too much in terms of money and/or resources?

The number of abortions reported to the Centers for Disease Control and Prevention from 1973 through 2018, detailed in three reports contained on their website, totaled over 46.5 million.[10, 11, 12] That's an average of more than one million abortions per year.

A 2020 report, "American War and Military Operations Casualties: Lists and Statistics," by the Congressional Research Service reports the deaths of soldiers who died during wartime from 1775 to 1991 totaled just over 1 million, excluding Confederate soldiers who died in the Civil War.[13]

Comparing these figures, the average number of abortions each year in America is about the same as all the deaths of American soldiers in all the US wars combined. Each human being is of great value to our Lord because every person bears his image. Therefore, God says, "And from each human being, too, I will demand an accounting for the life of another human being. Whoever sheds human blood, by humans shall their blood be shed; for in the image of God has God made humankind" (Genesis 9:5–6). When God created the earth and everything in it, he placed humankind in charge to rule over his creation. God has called us to be faithful stewards over all he has created, including caring for each other.

In 2007, when professional football player Michael Vick was sentenced to prison for running a dogfighting ring, I remember considering the irony of his sentence. Certainly, the treatment of animals in such barbaric fashion should not go unpunished, but where is the consistency of our justice system in America today? In our current legal system, a person can be imprisoned for treating dogs inhumanely, yet aborting more than one million babies a year is legal and acceptable. Our system protects animals who can't speak in their own defense but doesn't protect unborn babies who are also unable to speak in their defense. Something seems badly skewed here. Isn't a human life at least as precious as an animal's life? How can politicians and lawmakers expect people to respect the sanctity of life when the laws they enact don't respect life?

I see an increasing propensity for individuals to give full vent to their rage by engaging in violence toward others, even if the victims are unknown to them. A report by the Federal Bureau of Investigation, "Active Shooter Incidents in the United States in 2019," states, "The FBI defines 'active shooter' as one or more individuals actively engaged in killing or attempting to kill people in a populated area with one or more firearms. The FBI has designated 28 shootings in 2019 as active shooter incidents . . . resulting in 97 people killed and 150 people wounded.[14]

Another article by the FBI, "Quick Look: 277 Active Shooter Incidents in the United States From 2000 to 2018," indicates the FBI identified 277 active shooter incidents in the US from 2008 to 2018, resulting in 884 deaths and 1,546 wounded.[15]

An April 2020 article by Dave Lawler & Orion Rummler, "The Deadliest Mass Shootings in Modern U.S. History," states, "The big picture: Mass shootings are becoming deadlier. The deadliest shooting 10 years ago left 16 people dead. The toll from the 2017 shooting at Las Vegas hotel is 59."[16] The numbers contained in this article can be summarized as follows. The 22 deadliest shootings, taking place during 1949 to 2019, a 70-year period, resulted in 446 deaths and 685 wounded. Thirteen of these events took place in one decade, from 2009 to 2019, resulting in 288 deaths and 668 wounded.

Many of us heard the news media broadcast the devastating details of some of these horrific events. As each incident unfolded, multiple news teams were present at the scene, seemingly camped out twenty-four hours a day, analyzing the facts and interviewing everyone who was willing to talk. In the aftermath, each news team focused on how such a thing could happen. The "Why?" question was the most prevalent by far. Many offered their conjectures.

Such a question is normal for everyone who wants to know how to keep themselves and their loved ones safe. It is also an important question for law enforcement as they attempt to determine how to prevent such violence in the future. However, one response to the question was almost nonexistent, which I found odd indeed. Hardly anyone offered "evil" as the reason for these actions. Do people not see evil as a viable reason for the increasing savagery? Or do they recognize the possibility but are reluctant to verbalize such thoughts? The earthly effects of evil in America (and everywhere else) are becoming more blatant with each passing day. Sanctity of life, love of family, and love of others seems to be decreasing significantly in America as time passes. Now it's my turn to ask "Why?" But it's a rhetorical question. I think I already know the answer.

Another type of violence, orchestrated under the guise of racial equality and fair treatment, is taking place in our homeland. Its purpose, in my opinion, is to marginalize or eliminate governmental authority and sow additional seeds of fear and chaos wherever possible. In May 2020, most of us watched TV in horror as George Floyd, a forty-six-year-old black male, died at the hands of Minneapolis police after being arrested. Floyd's death sparked protests, rioting, and looting. It is important to make a clear distinction here. Many Americans of every ethnic group were gathering around the nation to peacefully protest the heinous acts leading to the death of George Floyd and, by extension, the oppressive treatment of any human in America, and rightly so. Our country's history of slavery and oppression of people of color is a grievous scar on the soul of our nation. However, those who are rioting and looting have motives completely removed from George Floyd's death. The violence and subversive motives being addressed here apply to the anarchistic criminal element who use the cover of the peaceful protestors to hide their cowardly acts of violence and lawlessness.

In the last half of 2020, after George Floyd's death, many of us saw the news coverage of widespread violence and destruction in cities across our country. A June 2020 article by Evita Duffy, "Capitol Hill Organized Protest: Vegan Utopia or Urban Anarchy?", states,

> A police precinct and six blocks of downtown Seattle's Capitol Hill district were taken over by Antifa and Black Lives Matter rioters. The area . . . has now officially been renamed the Capitol Hill Organized Protest (CHOP) . . . Allies in the media aided in spinning the image of anarchist squatters into harmless "protesters," but social media footage tells another story. Namely, forcibly removing the police and erecting border fencing . . . Despite reports of violence and looting . . . the mayor of Seattle has referred to CHOP as a harmless "block party" and predicted the coming months in CHOP would be "the summer of love." Meanwhile, in the absence of law enforcement, armed citizens are policing the streets.[17]

Demonstrators across the country have been calling for defunding the police. Astoundingly, numerous city governments, including those in New York City and Los Angeles, our two largest cities, have acted on or are considering reductions in their police departments' budgets. Such actions play into the hands of those with a subversive agenda who want to replace law and order with mob rule. Meanwhile, the riots, protests, and number of people injured or killed continue to grow as weeks and months pass.

According to a Justice News release on July 28, 2020, Attorney General William Barr testified before the House Judiciary Committee stating,

> Some have chosen to respond to George Floyd's death in a far less productive way—by demonizing the police . . . and making grossly irresponsible proposals to defund the police . . . When a community turns on and pillories its own police, officers naturally become more risk averse and crime rates soar. Unfortunately, we are seeing that now in many of our major cities . . . In the wake of George Floyd's death, violent rioters and anarchists have hijacked legitimate protests to wreak senseless havoc and destruction on innocent victims. The current situation in Portland is a telling example. Every night for the past two months, a mob of hundreds of rioters has laid siege to the federal courthouse and other nearby federal property. The rioters arrive equipped for a fight, armed with powerful slingshots, tasers, sledgehammers, saws, knives, rifles, and explosives. Inside the courthouse are a relatively small number of federal law enforcement personnel charged with a defensive mission: to protect the courthouse from being overrun and destroyed.[18]

A Department of Justice article summarizes an op-ed from July 27, 2020, by Brian T. Moran, US Attorney for the Western District of Washington, stating,

> Some city council members have seized on this moment of reflection to push their agenda to 'defund the police.' While there is no clear agreement of what 'defunding the police' looks like in Seattle, a majority of the city council has committed to cutting 50% from the police department's budget . . . For a number of weeks, the country watched while we engaged in an experiment called the Capitol Hill Occupied Protest (CHOP). We saw the human impact of Seattle's 'hands off CHOP' policy play out in deadly fashion. Two young black men were killed; crime rose 525%, according to Mayor Jenny

Durkan; and 911 calls went unheeded or responses were greatly delayed. Put simply, CHOP quickly devolved into chaos because police were absent.[19]

I am reminded of a young American who, many years ago, commented publicly on similar dangerous developments, such as mob rule, taking place in his beloved homeland. He said,

> By the operation of this mobocractic spirit, which all must admit, is now abroad in the land, the strongest bulwark of any government, and particularly of those constituted like ours, may effectually be broken down and destroyed . . . Whenever this effect shall be produced among us; whenever the vicious portion of population shall be permitted to gather in bands of hundreds and thousands, and burn churches, ravage and rob provision-stores, throw printing presses into rivers, shoot editors, and hang and burn obnoxious persons at pleasure, and with impunity; depend on it, this government cannot last . . . There is no grievance that is a fit object of redress by mob law . . . The question recurs, "How shall we fortify against it?" The answer is simple. Let every American, every lover of liberty, every well-wisher to his posterity, swear by the blood of the Revolution, never to violate in the least particular, the laws of the country; and never to tolerate their violation by others.[20]

The young man was Abraham Lincoln, and the year was 1838. Are there any similarities between what he saw then and what we are witnessing today?

Evil actions by humans and Satan's influence are not the only causes of chaos in America. Nature has played a role as well. I'm not sure if natural disasters are occurring more frequently today or if technological improvements in communication make it easier to report these events as they are happening. Either way, it seems like I hear about epidemics, earthquakes, and other natural calamities around the world with increasing regularity. Oddly enough, famines, which occur often in Africa and some other parts of the world, don't get much coverage by the American press. In recent years, our media has placed great emphasis on severe weather events. This may or may not be to promote their theory of manmade climate change.

One senator in particular has ranted about how humankind needs to preserve earth's resources and is destroying earth by ignoring climate change. It's almost as if this person believes we have some kind of godlike power over the fate of our planet. We did not create the world, nor will we destroy it. Before God formed the world, he already knew the day he would destroy it. However, the senator is right in at least two respects. First, God expects believers to serve as good stewards of everything he has provided to us for our survival and benefit. This includes air, water, soil, and the other natural resources we enjoy on earth. Second, climate change in the end is a fact. The planet will get infinitely hotter by the time the Lord returns. Scripture tells us, "But the day of the Lord will come like a thief. The heavens will disappear with a roar; the elements will be destroyed by fire, and the earth and everything done in it will be laid bare (2 Peter 3:10).

Our world has experienced numerous pandemics over the last century, with devastating results. The Centers for Disease Control and Prevention recorded the following major events.

- The 1918 influenza pandemic was the most severe in recent history. It infected about one third of the world's population, resulting in at least 50 million deaths worldwide, with approximately 675,000 deaths occurring in the United States.[21]
- The 1957 "Asian Flu" influenza virus caused an estimated 1.1 million deaths worldwide, with 116,000 of those in the United States.[22]
- The 1968 influenza virus caused an estimated 1 million deaths worldwide, with about 100,000 in the United States.[23]
- The 2009 influenza virus caused between 151,700 and 575,400 deaths worldwide during the first year the virus circulated. An estimated 60.8 million people were infected, resulting in more than 12,000 deaths in the United States.[24]
- Since 1981, acquired immunodeficiency syndrome (AIDS), caused by the human immunodeficiency virus (HIV), has resulted in an estimated 65 million infections and 25 million deaths worldwide.[25]
- There have been an estimated 1.2 million AIDS/HIV infections and 692,789 deaths in the United States.[26]

- In late 2019, COVID-19, an infectious disease, broke out in Wuhan, China. In February 2020, three patients were hospitalized with this virus in the state of Washington, and one died, resulting in the first known COVID-19 death in the United States.[27]
- According to the Centers for Disease Control, as of March 29, 2021, there have been approximately 30,095,827 COVID-19 cases and 546,704 deaths in America.[28]
- According to the World Health Organization, as of March 29, 2021, there have been 126,697,603 confirmed cases of COVID-19, including 2,776,175 deaths, reported to them.[29]

The number of COVID-19 cases and deaths continue to increase daily. As a result of this pandemic, I experienced several things for the first time in my life. A huge percentage of the American economy was shut down, resulting in tens of millions of workers being laid off, either temporarily or permanently. Everyone was asked to work from home if possible and to stay home except for essential travel (going to the doctor, pharmacy, or grocery). School-age children were obtaining their schooling at home. Churches were asked, and in some states ordered, to close. Everyone was asked, and in some states ordered, to wear masks if travel outside the home was required.

Chaos appears to be increasing daily, originating from a variety of sources. For many people, these are scary times, but those who study and believe God's Word knew this chaos was coming. We simply didn't know when. We also know the reason for the mayhem. We need to be calm and assured in this time of fear. Then, when given an opportunity, we can provide God's answer to those who have questions, explaining the hope that resides within us.

CHAPTER 9

The Struggle Against Spiritual Forces

> For our struggle is not against flesh and blood, but against the rulers, against the authorities, against the powers of this dark world and against the spiritual forces of evil in the heavenly realms. (Ephesians 6:12)

We have looked at the struggles with self and other people regarding our spiritual lives. Everyone, saved or unsaved, in their sinful nature desires what is contrary to God. After a critical naval victory against the British on Lake Erie in 1813, Commodore Oliver Perry sent a dispatch stating, "We have met the enemy and they are ours."[1] Some say this dispatch is the origin for a well-known quote, "We have met the enemy, and he is us." As we examine the spiritual war raging around us, we must ask ourselves, "Who is the enemy?" As soldiers in the Lord's army, we need to ensure we have properly identified the primary foe, so we can effectively strategize on how to defeat them. Is flesh and blood the true enemy? Scripture says, "No!" Satan is the true enemy of God, desiring to replace him.

In his book, *The Gathering Storm*, Dr. Albert Mohler states, "That is the challenge faced by Christians in the United States today—to see the storm and to understand it, and then to demonstrate the courage to face the storm. We must see the storm and understand it, if we are to be faithful to Christ in this secular age."[2] We must recognize and understand the storm. Is there any doubt in your mind a full-fledged spiritual war is raging all around us? The legal, moral, and social battles involving abortion, freedom of religion and speech, gay rights, orphans, pornography, poverty, racism, and sexual slavery, just to name a few, are not simply ideological battles. These are spiritual battles as well. Satan encourages, enables, and assists everyone who opposes any biblical doctrine, including such foundational issues as humans being created in God's image, the worship of God, marriage, and family. The devil wants as many people as possible to oppose:

- any public display or expression of glory to God or his Son, Jesus;
- anyone who says marriage should be between one man and one woman for a lifetime;
- any definition of family as consisting of one man and one woman (husband and wife) with or without children; and
- the sanctity of life because humans are created in the image of God.

The stakes are high in this spiritual war because eternal souls hang in the balance. Satan has won numerous important battles right here in our homeland. The rate of these changes is increasing, like a rock rolling downhill, gathering speed. I am not claiming Lucifer is the cause of all the chaos in our homeland. I am fully capable of committing wrongful and even heinous acts because of my sinful nature. I don't need Satan's help. However, the great deceiver encourages and promotes any evil when given the opportunity. He encourages chaos because he knows it produces fear in the masses, and fear generates vulnerability. The greater the chaos Satan can help generate, the greater the rips and tears will be in the moral fabric of our society. Like human warfare, spiritual warfare is violent, ugly, and fraught with casualties. Another simple truth is, we cannot opt out of this war. It is in our homes as well as the homes of our friends and relatives. Most importantly, this war is taking place in every human soul.

Some Christians may not want to speak publicly about demons and spiritual warfare, believing others may consider them fanatical or crazy for taking such things seriously. Satan loves the silence of believers, but those who love Jesus Christ know spiritual warfare between the great dragon and God is both real and deadly. If the serpent can undermine or discredit the truth, it will be easier for him to ensnare more souls. Throughout history, two things have remained constant: God and Satan. Christians know the great deceiver will lose the war. We have read God's Word, and we know Lucifer's end, but the devil has no intention of quitting the battle. Satan is doggedly committed to fight until the bitter end. He also understands his single-most important battle is to erode the foundation of our faith. Therefore, he has attacked the truth, God's Word. From the conversation with Eve in the Garden of Eden until today, Satan has concentrated all his resources and his full fury on this endeavor. As a result, he has won significant battles and gained substantial ground in this arena. To the victor belong the spoils, which, in this case, are human souls. The truth, God's Word, is at the heart of this spiritual war.

What Is Truth?

The answer to this question depends on the respondent. About two thousand years ago in Jerusalem, the Jewish leaders took Jesus to Pilate, hoping to obtain Jesus's death sentence. During the ensuing conversation, Pilate said,

> "You are a king, then!"
>
> Jesus answered, "You say that I am a king. In fact, the reason I was born and came into the world is to testify to the truth. Everyone on the side of truth listens to me."
>
> "What is truth?" retorted Pilate. With this he went out again to the Jews gathered there and said, "I find no basis for a charge against him" (John 18:37–38).

Many people in every generation have been seeking the answer to Pilate's three-word question, "What is truth?" In Pilate's case, I find the brief conversation simultaneously profound and pitiful. It is profound because it is one of the most basic questions of life, though I presume Pilate was being facetious when he asked it. The question is also profound because Pilate asked it of the only human on earth who knew the answer perfectly. It is pitiful because this learned, powerful man of the world asked "What is truth?" while staring into the very eyes of the truth. Did Pilate fail to see the truth of Jesus's identity, or did he conveniently deny it? Scripture doesn't tell us. Either way, what could have been a life-changing encounter for Pilate passed him by without notice.

The Bible tells us God's Word, (John 17:17), Jesus Christ (John 14:6), and the Holy Spirit (John 14:17) are truth. God also describes his Word as God-breathed, perfect, flawless, eternal, and never failing. Scripture provides a direct answer to the question, "What is truth?" But how would others answer? If you posed this question to a Hindu, a Buddhist, a Jew, a Muslim, a Scientologist, an agnostic, and an atheist, you would get seven very different answers. In fact, if you posed this question to seven different Christians, you might get as many as seven different answers.

Increasing Opposition to the Truth

America has more diversity in religion today than when I was a child. I'm not speaking only of non-Christian religions, such as Buddhism, Hinduism, and Islam. I never heard of the Church of Satan, Scientology, Santeria, New Age, paganism, and wicca until I was an adult. These groups may have existed in America when I was a child, but if so, they were unknown to me. Along with the increasing number of non-Christian religions in our country today, a growing portion of Americans don't want to hear what Christians have to say about God's Word or how people should live. These groups include those who:

- Already subscribe to a faith other than Christianity;
- Hold to no faith at all;
- Support or subscribe to "alternative" lifestyles;
- Seek to establish their own "truth" based on their wants and desires; or
- Hold the reins of power and don't want Christians "inciting the masses."

When you "get down to brass tacks," as my Mom used to say, the only two groups of people in America who are interested in hearing about God's Word are Christians and those unsaved who are truly searching for the truth. Everyone else would prefer we just shut up and go away. This opposition, whether organizational or individual, takes different forms, including, denial, suppression, and persecution.

Denial of the Truth

Is there more than one truth? Do all paths lead to heaven? As time passes, it seems fewer people in America subscribe to God's Word as the absolute truth.

According to research conducted in July 2015 by the Barna Group, Christian morality is being ushered out of American social structures and off the cultural main stage, leaving a vacuum in its place, and the broader culture is attempting to fill the void. This research reveals growing concern about the nation's moral condition, even as many American adults admit they are uncertain about how to determine right from wrong. Here are some of their findings.

- Eighty percent of American adults (90 percent of Christians) across age groups, ethnicities, genders, socioeconomic status, and political ideology express concern about the nation's moral condition.
- Forty-one percent of practicing Christians agree the only truth one can know is whatever is right for one's own life.
- Practicing Christians (59 percent) are nearly four times more likely than adults with no faith (15 percent) to believe moral truth is absolute.
- Americans are concerned about the nation's moral condition and confused about morality itself. Barna's research reveals the degree to which Americans pledge allegiance to the "morality of self-fulfillment," a new moral code that, as David Kinnaman, President of Barna Group, argues, has all but replaced Christianity as the culture's moral norm.[3]

I talked earlier about Christians who don't believe the Holy Bible is the inerrant Word of God. It also makes perfect sense to me that the overwhelming majority of non-believers (85 percent) establish their own moral code as they see fit. Nor do they care to hear anything to the contrary. In his book, *The Gathering Storm*, Dr. Albert Mohler warns, "The secular age exerts a subtle but constant influence on churches and Christians. If not careful, churches will look less and less like churches and more and more like the secular world around them . . . Liberal theology begins to slowly replace orthodox faith. Or . . . churches simply stop talking about or teaching important truths revealed in the Bible. The demand is to just be quiet."[4]

Some believers are vocal in the wrong way. There are Christian church leaders who publicly contradict God's Word. In a May 2019 article, "No, Christianity Doesn't Need to Endorse Homosexuality to Grow," Glenn T. Stanton wrote,

> Stop accepting the Bible as true and admit Christianity has gotten it terribly wrong on homosexuality. This is the

advice Rev. Oliver Thomas gives . . . for how the church can stop 'hemorrhaging members' and see brighter days. He warns that 'the church is killing itself' . . . by actually believing what the Bible says. He contends that Christians should just admit that the Bible gets it wrong on so many important issues and that "reason and experience" should be our new guide . . . He says the church is terribly wrong about sexuality, particularly homosexuality, and would do very well to wise up . . . "Churches will continue hemorrhaging members and money at an alarming rate until we muster the courage to face the truth: We got it wrong on gays and lesbians."[5]

Alexander Griswold, in an April 2014 article, "Adam Hamilton: Parts of Bible Don't Reflect God's Will," wrote about a speech given to a group by Adam Hamilton, pastor of the largest United Methodist congregation in the country, regarding his newest book. Hamilton said,

"The Bible was inspired by God, not verbally dictated as many believe . . . Every verse in the Bible that people found confusing or troubling fit into one of three "buckets" . . . The largest bucket was composed of . . . metaphors, such as the Creation story. The second largest bucket was verses that were relevant for a certain time and place, but no longer apply to Christians today, such as much of the Mosaic Law. But third was Hamilton's assertion that very few parts of the Bible 'never ever reflected the heart and character of God.'"[6]

Satan is always ready to do anything he can to help people decide to establish any "truth" other than God's Word. Maybe Christians do the same thing with Scripture sometimes. Maybe we want to believe what our high school science book said and believe in the Bible too. I tried that. It doesn't work. Both cannot be right. Maybe we want God's Word to say, or not say, certain things, so we can rest assured we will make it to heaven one day. I would certainly feel more comfortable with God being, all-loving and having no wrath and all-merciful and requiring no justice. I would also welcome the prospect of eternity in heaven with no risk of hell. But I cannot draw those conclusions from Scripture. I am convinced my choice in this matter is binary. I must either accept or reject all of God's Word as truth. Scripture does not allow me a "partially true" option. Our Lord says all Scripture is God-breathed. It is impossible for God to lie. If I start taking parts I don't like out of the Bible, it is no longer God's Word. I have altered it to become "my word," at which time I have entered the world of relativism.

With relativism, truth is in the eye of the beholder. It is whatever each person decides it is. Absolutes do not exist since a definition may change depending on a person's circumstance or feelings. Relativism is extremely dangerous because of the underlying forces motivating it: my internal desires and the devil's spiritual war against me. The deepest part of my self-centered psyche desires relativism when it comes to truth. My fallen nature screams, "I am in charge! I will make the rules for my life!" I desire truth to be relative, to be all about me. Relativism is nothing more than self-worship and self-deception. It has been around for as long as humans have existed. Satan is the author of deception. Relativism is just one tool the devil employs in his campaign to deny the truth of God's Word. He started with Eve in the Garden of Eden.

Scripture tells us the first words the great deceiver spoke to Eve were in the form of a question, "Did God really say, 'You must not eat from any tree in the garden?'" (Genesis 3:1). Satan attempted several things with this question. First, by asking "Did God really say," he was trying to place doubt in Eve's mind regarding the accuracy of God's words. This question implies two possibilities. Either God mis-stated what he said, or Eve misunderstood the meaning of God's words. Second, by inserting into the question "any tree in the garden," rather than the one tree God had specifically placed off limits (Genesis 2:17), the devil, as he often does, mixed a partial truth with his own lie to distort God's words. If Eve hadn't paid close attention to the instructions Adam received from God, she might not have caught the subtle change inserted into the question. Furthermore, the question, as posed by Lucifer, may also have been intended to imply an all-loving, gracious God wouldn't put all these luscious fruit trees in the garden if Eve was not supposed to eat from them.

However, Eve was paying attention when Adam relayed God's instructions, and her response was right on the mark. "The woman said to the serpent, 'We may eat fruit from the trees in the garden, but God did say, "You must not eat fruit from the tree that is in the middle of the garden, and you must not touch it, or you will die"'" (Genesis 3:3). Eve understood the serpent had misstated the truth. So, she simply repeated God's words on the subject, a tactic Jesus used many years later when he interacted with the devil in the wilderness. We will never go wrong if our responses are directly from God's Word, applied in context and delivered with humility in love. Furthermore, Eve's response correctly points out Lucifer's misstatement without accusing him. By his first question, Eve knew—or certainly should have known—the serpent was up to no good.

Satan knew from Eve's response that he would not achieve his goal by simply challenging the accuracy of God's word or Eve's understanding of the meaning. He would need to change tactics to succeed in his mission. An additional handicap was, at least two of Lucifer's favorite tools, guilt and shame, were not available for him to use against Eve. Since there had been no sin on earth, there was no guilt or shame (Genesis 2:25). So, the devil decided to challenge God's words, using a partial truth and a lie again, attempting to plant the seed of pride in Eve while offering a plausible reason why God might have been less than forthright with her.

"'You will not certainly die,' the serpent said to the woman. 'For God knows that when you eat from it your eyes will be opened, and you will be like God, knowing good and evil'" (Genesis 3:4–5). The truth the serpent told Eve was she would "know good and evil" if she ate of the tree. At this point in human history, neither Adam nor Eve knew evil. Eve had no need to "know evil." God was trying to protect her from such knowledge and prevent sin from entering the world. The devil's lie to Eve was "you will not certainly die."

I assume Lucifer knew Eve would not die an immediate physical death if she ate from the tree. Of course, he didn't bother to tell Eve she would certainly die a physical death eventually, since by eating the fruit she would sin and death would enter the world (Romans 5:12). Nor did he tell Eve she would certainly die a spiritual death because her sin would separate her from God. Satan also told Eve when she ate of the tree she "would be like God." Eve was already like God to the extent she was created in his image. She lived in intimate communion with him in a luscious garden where all her needs were met. Her home was nearly perfect, except for the serpent. After eating the fruit of the tree, Eve, because she had sinned, would be less like God than before she ate the fruit when she was sinless.

By twisting God's words, the great deceiver's explanation was designed not only to minimize the danger and consequences of disobeying God's command but also to show eating the forbidden fruit was of great pleasure and advantage to Eve. To sweeten the deception, Lucifer attempted to introduce discontent in Eve by pandering to her pride, telling her when she ate of the fruit she would "be like God," "knowing good and evil." Satan was intimately familiar with the pride of wanting to be like God. It led to his downfall (Isaiah 14:12–14). First, the serpent questioned the accuracy of God's command. Second, he contradicted God's words with a partial truth and a lie. This is his modus operandi to start us down the "path of untruth." Satan attempted to create doubt by contradicting God's command with a partial truth, hoping for a subsequent denial of God's words by Eve. The result was Eve, and then Adam, willingly made their choice (Genesis 3:6–7). The rest, as they say, is history.

We shouldn't overestimate our adversary, or we may become frozen with fear while denying the power of God residing within us. Nor should we underestimate our adversary since this may produce pride and complacency. The devil is not all-knowing or all-powerful. However, give him his due. He is smart, powerful, and extremely cunning, particularly compared to humans. Satan was willing to tempt Jesus for forty days and nights in the wilderness. Do you really think he has any fear of you or me? He is neither clumsy nor stupid. He is subtle, articulate, and persuasive. He doesn't try to sway us by telling us the Bible is totally false. He works gradually, starting with one small part of Scripture to get us to question the accuracy of one thing, just like he did with Eve. Once Lucifer has gotten us to doubt one part of Scripture, he will start on another part of Scripture later.

Sometimes he twists Scripture to give it another meaning, as we saw with Eve. Other times he uses God's Word, guilt, and twisted logic to encourage sin. The great deceiver may also start with one "small sin" by whispering, "It's OK this one time." Once we become comfortable with the one "small sin," he entices us to engage in the next "small sin" and so on. The serpent knew he needed to be subtle and wily in his interaction with Eve. The insinuation of sin into her life had to be handled deftly. The devil will use every ploy method available to detract glory from God. He is a master fisherman who knows the best bait to entice each one of us. For some, the message must be subtle. For others, a brazen message will work. Satan is a liar and the father of lies (John 8:44). He is truly the best deceiver who has ever existed.

Suppression of the Truth

Denial is not the only instrument in Lucifer's spiritual toolbelt that he uses against God's Word. Suppression is another powerful implement he uses every chance he gets. As soon as the gospel message was presented to the world, suppression of that message began. The Jewish leaders conspired with the Roman authorities to have Jesus wrongfully put to death. Much to their dismay, the Jewish leaders were then faced with Jesus's empty tomb, another miracle to add to an already impressive list. So, the chief priests and elders conspired with the Roman government again to hide the truth. The Jewish leaders agreed to pay the soldiers who guarded the tomb a large sum of money if they would say, "Jesus's disciples came during the night and stole his body." The Jewish leaders also promised to protect the soldiers if this story got back to the Roman governor (Matthew 28:12–15).

As Christianity spread from its origin in Judea and Galilee throughout the world, suppression of God's truth followed. Satan is still perpetuating his worldwide war against God's Word. Suppression of the truth, perpetrated by a variety of people and institutions, has continued to occur in the present. Skirmishes over religious freedom existed in America even before our nation was officially formed. More recently, an ideological war has been brewing for decades at least. In the past few years, this war seems to have increased exponentially, spilling onto Main Street, USA, with significant coverage in the press. The two camps involved in this fracas are referred to as the "liberal left" or "far left" and the "religious right" or "far right." Each group has very different ideas regarding what constitutes free speech versus hate speech and freedom of religion versus religious intolerance. These phrases are currently at the forefront of America's conversations. It seems to have taken on a different meaning than what I was taught. The divide in America over these ideologies, particularly over the past decade, is widening, producing more polarization, hostility, and violence.

College campuses are not immune to this polarization or its negative effects. In recent years, rioting has broken out on college campuses as militant activists have attempted to shut down what they consider to be provocative speakers whose views they oppose. I am convinced the most fundamental underlying issue is not what constitutes free speech or hate speech. Historically, colleges and universities have been known for their acceptance of novel thinking and free expression of thoughts, even if they differ from the ideas of others.

It seems a new "relative" definition of free speech is arising in America. For some of those who are attending college, free speech is defined as "speech agreeable to them." Any speech to the contrary is to be suppressed, silenced by whatever means, including violence, under the guise that such speech is really hate speech or intolerant. Many voices in America today are calling for religious opinions to be tolerant or non-offensive. For many who support such views, this is simply another way of them telling people not to say anything in public that offends others. However, the same rules do not apply to the makers of this rule. They can say whatever they want even if it offends others. They consider themselves to be the ones to determine what can and cannot be expressed.

"Shouting down" is another tactic that is becoming more frequently employed by those who disagree with a particular message or point of view. An April 2018 article by College Fix, "11 times campus speakers were shouted down by leftist protesters this school year," states, "It's been another banner year for leftists who refuse to allow free speech on campus. It's their way, or the highway. Who are the real fascists?. . . And there's no end in sight."[7]

Protesting students are not the only group attempting to engage in curtailment of free speech on college campuses. Institutional censorship is another technique used to silence opposition. Some of those who oversee college campuses have engaged in censorship of free speech as well, under the guise of tolerance, inclusion, or "campus speech codes." According to a Justice News release on September 17, 2018, Acting Assistant Attorney General John Gore spoke at the Justice Department's forum on Free Speech in Higher Education, stating,

> "Today the country faces a new challenge to free speech in a new forum. Ironically, this forum once served as the incubator of free speech - but today, it far too often has become an inhibitor of free and open discourse. I speak, of course, of institutions of higher education . . . Instead of empowering students to expand their minds in the marketplace of ideas, these misguided administrators and faculty have enfeebled students to seek refuge from intellectual debate in the confines of campus speech codes . . . To date, we have filed statements of interest

in four cases challenging unconstitutional campus speech codes."⁸

Another tactic, called "cancel culture," is used to suppress free speech when someone doesn't like what they hear. The idea is to silence anyone who has an opposing idea or position. I watched as President Trump, at the Turning Point Action Convention in Phoenix, Arizona, on June 23, 2020, introduced Reagan Escude, who briefly recounted her experience with the cancel culture after posting a video on Instagram regarding the church's response to the Black Lives Matter movement. In her speech, Reagan stated, "Racism is a problem in the heart. It is a sin problem that cannot be resolved by any law, protest, or march." Escude explained that a former co-worker and others accused her of being racist and homophobic because of her video. After Reagan's employer received death threats, Reagan was fired from her job. She told the audience in Phoenix, "Losing my job is a small price to pay when God's name is being glorified. And he will always make his name known. This is one example of something happening on a large scale in America."⁹

We also see our elected government officials exerting the power of their political positions to stop the words and actions of those they oppose. *Christian Post* reporter Michael Gryboski, in a May 2013 article, "Franklin Graham: IRS Targeted Samaritan's Purse, Billy Graham Evangelistic Association," writes,

> Evangelist Franklin Graham sent a letter to President Obama . . . outlining how Samaritan's Purse and the Billy Graham Evangelistic Association were the subjects of an IRS probe during the 2012 campaign season . . . Last week the Internal Revenue Service acknowledged that it had targeted conservative organizations applying for tax exemption under section 501(c)4 . . . Lois Lerner, head of the IRS division that oversees tax-exempt organizations, apologized for the biased targeting of groups whose applications involved terms like "Tea Party" or "Patriot."¹⁰

This was not the first time Franklin Graham, a Christian, found himself at odds with some portion of the US government regarding his faith. Jeff Schogol, in an April 2010 article, "Army withdraws Franklin Graham Pentagon prayer day invitation," writes,

> The Army has disinvited Franklin Graham to speak at the Pentagon on National Prayer Day after a military advocacy group objected because Graham has reportedly described Islam as "evil" and "wicked" . . . Graham was expected to speak at the Pentagon on May 6, drawing the ire of the Military Religious Freedom Foundation, a watchdog group focused on religious favoritism in the military. The group had been prepared to seek a temporary restraining order against National Prayer Day if it were "polluted by someone as hideously Islamophobic as Franklin Graham," said Mikey Weinstein, head of the group.[11]

Today, some politicians are openly advocating harassment, another tool used to silence those who hold differing political views. In June 2020, I watched news media coverage of representative Maxine Waters, who was calling on her supporters to confront Trump administration officials and staffers in public. Waters told the crowd, "If you see anybody from the cabinet you tell them they're not welcome anymore, anywhere." Have we seen the last vestiges of civility among our nation's leaders? If so, a significant portion of the populace could quickly follow suit.

Legal action has also been taken by groups or individuals to suppress or silence the opposition regarding religious matters. The First Amendment to the US Constitution says, "Congress shall make no law respecting an establishment of religion, or prohibiting the free exercise thereof; or abridging the freedom of speech, or of the press; or the right of the people peaceably to assemble, and to petition the Government for a redress of grievance."[12]

Volumes of articles and books have been written on this topic. Those who hold fast to the constitutional principles of freedom of speech and freedom of religion say people can talk about their faith anytime, anywhere. Those who don't want to hear any rhetoric they oppose, particularly the truth of God's Word, rely on separation of church and state or the notion that religious speech is intolerant or offensive to restrict speech. Those who want all religious expression confined to the four walls of a building of worship are aggressively utilizing the court system to impose their desires. The ultimate objective is to stop anyone from saying anything publicly about God or Jesus. They will get what they want sooner or later. Randy Allen, senior minister at Bethel Church of Christ in Ada, Ohio, once said while preaching, "For those who have lived their entire lives wanting God to be absent from it, He will give them exactly what they desired; an eternity without him."

When I entered grade school, each day began with the teacher leading the students in the Pledge of Allegiance and a prayer to God in the name of Jesus Christ. These practices would end soon. An article by Findlaw on the case of Engel v. Vitale (1962) states, "The United States Supreme Court ruled the First Amendment, made applicable to state law through the Fourteenth Amendment, bars state sponsored prayer recitations in public schools".[13]

Another article by Findlaw on the Supreme Court case Abington School District v. Schempp, 374 U.S. 203 (1963) states, "The Court held that school-sponsored Bible reading constituted government endorsement of a particular religion, and thus violated the Establishment Clause of the First Amendment."[14]

In an August 2003 article, "The Controversy Over Alabama's Ten Commandments Statue, And the Nature of Justified Civil Disobedience," Anthony J. Sebok writes,

> "Chief Justice Roy Moore was suspended from his position as a member of the Alabama Supreme Court . . . Previously, a local federal district court judge had ordered Moore to remove the Ten Commandments statue, on the ground that it violated the U.S. Constitution's First Amendment . . . Justice Moore appealed, but the U.S. Court of Appeals for the Fifth Circuit and the United States Supreme Court both rejected his appeals. Nevertheless, Moore decided to ignore the court order, and leave the statue where it was . . . Accordingly, Moore was suspended."[15]

An August 2013 *Christian News* article, "New Orleans City Council Officially Lifts Ban on Preaching After Sundown," states,

> "New Orleans City Council . . . enacted the 'Aggressive Solicitation' ordinance in 2011, which banned all evangelistic activity and free speech from sunset to sunrise on Bourbon Street. This past week, the New Orleans City Council voted 6-0 to amend the ordinance which had been

suspended by a U.S. District Judge . . . in September . . . The city council revised the ordinance at the request of another U.S. District Judge who is currently weighing the legality of the ban after multiple street preachers were either arrested or threatened with arrest at the Southern Decadence festival in 2012."[16]

According to a Justice News release, on October 11, 2019, Attorney General William Barr spoke at the law school at Notre Dame University stating,

"I think we all recognize that over the past fifty years, religion has been under increasing attack. On one hand we have seen the steady erosion of our traditional Judeo-Christian moral system and a comprehensive effort to drive it from the public square. On the other hand, we see the ascendency of secularism and the doctrine of moral relativism. By any honest assessment, the consequences of this moral upheaval have been grim. Virtually every measure of social pathology continues to gain ground . . . Secularists, and their allies among the "progressives," have marshalled all the forces of mass communication, popular culture, the entertainment industry and academia in an unremitting assault on religion and traditional values. The instruments are used not only to affirmatively promote secular orthodoxy, but also to drown out and silence opposing voices and to attack viciously, and hold up to ridicule, any dissenters."[17]

These are the words of our leading law enforcement officer in America. A significant portion of Americans do not want anyone telling them anything about Jesus Christ. This is nothing new for our Lord. Several thousand years ago, God spoke through the prophet Jeremiah, saying, "To whom can I speak and give warning? Who will listen to me? Their ears are closed so they cannot hear. "The word of the Lord is offensive to them; they find no pleasure in it" (Jeremiah 6:10). On another occasion the Lord spoke through the prophet Isaiah, saying, "Truth is nowhere to be found, and whoever shuns evil becomes a prey" (Isaiah 59:15).

THE STRUGGLE AGAINST SPIRITUAL FORCES

Luke Goodrich, an attorney for the Becket Fund for Religious Liberty, has spent more than a decade protecting religious freedom for people of all faiths. He has been involved in victories in four Supreme Court cases and many more lower court cases. In his book, *Free to Believe: The Battle over Religious Liberty in America,* Goodrich says, "American Christians haven't faced serious violations of their religious freedom for a long time, but much of Scripture was written to Christians who were facing just that. To live our faith in modern culture, we need to reclaim and reacquaint ourselves with what Scripture says to the persecuted church."[18] Goodrich continues, "Now our culture has changed. For the first time in American history, common Christian beliefs are viewed as incompatible with the prevailing culture. Like other religious minorities before us, we're viewed as a threat."[19]

Those who are viewed as a threat will be treated as a threat. However, non-believers are not the only ones who engage in suppression of the truth. At times it originates within the religious community. An article in the Christian Classics Ethereal Library, "Bible Reading by the Laity, Restrictions On," can be summarized as follows.

- In 1880, Pope John VIII permitted a translation of the Latin gospel into Slavonic. However, in 1080, Pope Gregory VII characterized the custom as unwise, bold, and forbidden.
- In 1229, the Synod of Toulouse forbade the laity to have in their possession any copy of the books of the Bible except the Psalter and some other portions of Scripture. They further ordered "We most strictly forbid these works in the vulgar." This was in response to criticism of the Catholic church by other groups.
- In 1234, the Synod of Tarragona ordered all vernacular versions of the Bible to be brought to the bishop to be burned.
- Similar decrees were made by King James I (1276) and Pope Paul II (1464–1471).
- Ferdinand and Isabella of Spain (1474–1516) prohibited the translation of the Bible into the vernacular or the possession of such translations.
- The Council of Trent in 1546 decreed it would be unlawful for anyone to print any books on sacred matters without them first being examined and approved by the Church.

- In 1530, Henry VIII of England made the reading of the Bible dependent on the permission of the superiors. William Tyndale's version, printed before 1535, was prohibited.
- The reason given for these restrictions was so the laity would not be injured. If the Bible was translated into the vulgar tongue and indiscriminately allowed to everyone, the "rashness of men" would cause more evil than good to arise from it.[20]

We must know the truth to understand how we are to live for God and to discern the lies of this world. The truth of God's Word is the sieve we are to use to filter every thought, word, and deed. Satan understands this, and he uses every means available to keep the Word of God out of people's hands and minds.

CHAPTER 10

Persecuting Messengers of The Truth

> Then you will be handed over to be persecuted and put to death, and you will be hated by all nations because of me. (Matthew 24:9)

Believers have been persecuted for their faith throughout history. Abel was murdered because his offering to God was better than Cain's. Many of God's prophets were killed for the message they brought to the people. Jesus was persecuted and crucified for his message of truth. Some of the earliest Christians were tortured, imprisoned, and killed for their faith in the Son of God. For those who put their faith in Jesus Christ as Lord and Savior and were willing to proclaim the good news, persecution was sure to follow. Over the centuries and into today, persecution has taken many forms, including ridiculing, ostracizing, social and economic discrimination, violence, imprisonment, and death. When one form of persecution does not produce the desired result, those who oppress resort to harsher methods until they achieve their goal.

In Jesus's Time

From the time of his birth, powerful people wanted Jesus dead. When the Magi came to find the king of the Jews, the Messiah, Herod tried to get them to report Jesus's location to him. When the Magi did not return to Herod with Jesus's location, Herod ordered all the boys in Bethlehem who were two years old and younger to be killed to ensure Jesus did not survive (Matthew 2:16). Some thirty years later when Jesus began his public ministry, the Jewish leaders took up the quest to see him killed. They hated Jesus because they feared his power and authority might usurp their position of honor within the Jewish community. The Bible recounts some of their plots against Jesus, including the following

- When Jesus went into the synagogue and healed a man's shriveled hand on the Sabbath, the Pharisees plotted how they might kill him (Matthew 12:13–14).
- When Jesus cleared the temple because of the money-changers, the chief priests and the teachers of the law began looking for a way to kill him, for they feared him, because the whole crowd was amazed at his teaching (Mark 11:15–18).
- Because Jesus was healing on the Sabbath and was even calling God his Father, making himself equal with God, the Jewish leaders tried even harder to kill him (John 5:16–18).

Many early Christians were persecuted or died for their faith in Jesus. Scripture gives us a few examples of people called to martyrdom.

- John the Baptist was arrested, imprisoned, and beheaded because he rebuked Herod the tetrarch for marrying Herodias, the wife of Herod's brother, Philip (Matthew 14:9-10).
- Certain Jews falsely accused Stephen of blasphemy against Moses and against God (Acts 6:11). When questioned by the Sanhedrin, Stephen accused them of murdering the Righteous One, Jesus Christ, and was stoned to death (Acts 7:59–60).

- King Herod, in order to persecute believers, had James, the brother of John and the son of Zebedee, arrested and put to death by the sword (Acts 12:1–3).
- The Sanhedrin ordered Peter and John not to preach in the name of Jesus Christ, but they refused to stop (Acts 4:18–20).
- The Sanhedrin gave the apostles strict orders not to preach in the name of Jesus Christ, but they refused to stop (Ac 5:28–29). The apostles were flogged, but they left rejoicing (Acts 5:40–41).
- Other Christians were tortured, flogged, imprisoned, stoned, sawed in two, or killed by the sword. They were destitute, persecuted, and mistreated. They lived in caves and holes in the ground (Hebrews 11:35–38).
- "Nero became Roman emperor in A.D. 54 succeeding his stepfather, Claudius, . . . During Nero's rule the Great Fire broke out in Rome (A.D. 64) . . . Nero . . . could not dispel the rumor that he had the fire set . . . He selected the Christians as his scapegoats . . . claiming they had set the fire. A systematic persecution of the Christians followed . . . Nero committed suicide . . . in A.D. 68."[1]
- "Festus succeeded Felix as procurator of Judea (Acts 24:27). He assumed this office at Nero's appointment in A.D. 60, holding it until his death in A.D. 62. Paul the apostle appealed to Porcius Festus for the opportunity of being tried before Caesar, and Festus granted that request."[2]
- Nero was Roman emperor during the events at the end of the book of Acts when Paul was under house arrest awaiting trial in Rome (Acts 28:16). According to Eusebius, "Thus, Nero publicly announcing himself as the chief enemy of God, was led on in his fury to slaughter the apostles. Paul is therefore said to have been beheaded at Rome and Peter to have been crucified under him."[3]
- Eusebius also writes that James, the half-brother of Jesus, was approached by the scribes and Pharisees to renounce Jesus publicly, so the people would not be led astray. When James publicly proclaimed Jesus from the top of the temple, he was thrown to the ground, stoned, and beaten with a club until dead.[4]

Strange people, these first-century Christians who died for their faith. Some might even call them peculiar. By the time Jesus Christ ascended into heaven, his followers understood Jesus had come to earth to die, so those who believed in him might have eternal life with him one day. Those who opposed Christianity hoped that killing Jesus and his earliest followers would eradicate Jesus's name and nullify his claims. These opponents failed to understand that no power could overcome this body of Christians, which Jesus had already started building.

Abroad

The Christians who had congregated in Jerusalem were scattered throughout Judea and Samaria following the murder of Stephen and subsequent persecution of believers (Acts 8:1–3). The good news of Jesus Christ was being preached as they went, to Jews and Gentiles alike (Acts 11:19–21). As God's Word was spread throughout additional parts of the world, persecution of Christians followed quickly into those areas. In the first century, much of the known world, including Judea and Galilee, was subject to the Roman Empire.

- A Christian History Institute article, "Christian History Timeline: Persecution in the Early Church," outlines significant persecution of Christians by numerous Roman emperors in the first four centuries; beginning with Nero in AD 64 through the Great Persecution beginning in AD 303 under Diocletian.[5]
- During the Middle Ages at least seven major conflicts took place between the Christians and Muslims, known as the Crusades or Holy Wars. The Catholic Church also initiated inquisitions in Europe that sought to suppress any opinion in opposition to Church doctrine.
- An article in the Christian Classics Ethereal Library, "Bible Reading by the Laity, Restrictions On," states in 1408 the Third Synod of Oxford, as a result of John Wycliffe's Bible translation, forbid the translation of any text of Scripture into English or the reading of any such book or treatise composed in the time of John Wycliffe under pain of excommunication. In 1584, Pope Pius IV published ten rules, the fourth of which said a person who, without the consent of the bishops or inquisitors in writing, read a Bible translated into the vul-

gar tongue would not receive absolution until he or she first delivered up said Bible.[6]
- John Wycliffe (1320–1384), a theologian and early proponent of reform in the Roman Catholic Church, initiated the first translation of the Bible into the English language. For him the Bible was the fundamental source of Christianity that was binding on all people. His desire was to furnish the Bible to the people in their mother tongue. Because of his stand on these topics, in 1415 the Council of Constance declared Wycliffe a heretic and under the ban of the Church. It was decreed his books be burned and his remains be exhumed and burned.[7]
- William Tyndale (1494–1536) was a theologian and scholar who translated the Bible into an early form of Modern English, taking advantage of Gutenberg's press. Besides translating the Bible, Tyndale also held and published views considered heretical by the Catholic Church and later by the Church of England, established by Henry VIII. Tyndale's translation was banned by the authorities. In 1536, Tyndale was tried and convicted of heresy and treason. Tyndale was then strangled and burnt at the stake.[8]

From the beginning of Christianity through to the present, violent atrocities have been committed against believers throughout the world, like a never-ending horror show. An article by Samuel Smith, "1,202 Nigerian Christians killed in first six months of 2020: NGO report," states,

> "A Nigerian civil society group estimates that 1,202 Christians have been killed in Nigeria in the first six months of 2020 by jihadists, radicalized herdsmen and others . . . 'Thousands of defenseless Christians who survived being hacked to death have also been injured and left in mutilated conditions with several of them crippled for life.'. . . Hundreds of Christian worship and learning centers have been destroyed or burnt; likewise thousands of dwelling houses, farmlands and other properties belonging to Christians."[9]

Open Doors has been serving persecuted Christians for more than sixty years and is now serving in more than sixty countries. Their World Watch List is an annual report on the global persecution of Christians, ranking the top fifty countries where Christians are persecuted for their faith. Their "World Watch List 2020" indicates:

- Two hundred and sixty million Christians experience high levels of persecution in the top fifty countries on the World Watch List.
- The most dangerous places for Christians to live are, in order of severity: North Korea, Afghanistan, Somalia, Libya, Pakistan, Eritrea, Sudan, Yemen, Iran, and India.
- If North Korean Christians are discovered, they are deported to labor camps as political criminals or even killed on the spot. Driven by the state, Christian persecution in North Korea is extreme, and meeting other Christians to worship is nearly impossible unless it's done in secrecy.
- Afghanistan is a tribal society, and loyalty to one's family, clan, and tribe are extremely important. In Afghanistan, it is illegal for people to leave Islam. Those who decide to follow Jesus do so in secret.
- Somalia remains mired in civil war, tribalism, and violent Islamic militancy. Conversion to Christianity is regarded as a betrayal of the family and clan. If Somalis are suspected of being converts, family members and clan leaders will harass, intimidate, and even kill them.
- Libyan Christians with a Muslim background face violent and intense pressure to renounce their faith before their families and the wider community. Freedom of speech, equal treatment of Christians, and recognition of the church do not exist. No churches are being built.[10]

Several organizations attempt to track the persecution and murder of Christians around the world because of their faith. Accurate estimates are difficult to obtain, but the information available seems to point in one direction. The worldwide persecution of Christians is increasing over time.

At Home

My early grade school teachers taught that America was founded on Christian principles by people who fled England to avoid religious persecution. This teaching was correct as far as it went. People came to America for a variety of reasons, including earning a living, obtaining land, representing a company seeking profitable trade relations in a new land, and freedom of religion. These settlers came from England, France, Germany, Ireland, Netherlands, Spain, and other countries. Our founding fathers desired to establish a nation based on godly principles. However, there is also a consistent record of decidedly unchristian behavior in our history. It seems some of those who fled religious persecution in Europe perpetrated their own religious persecution in America against anyone who had differing religious beliefs. Each religious sect believed theirs was the only acceptable way to worship God.

An article, "Toleration in Old and New England, 3 June 1772," originally printed in *The London Packet* on June 3, 1772, states,

> "If we look back into history for the character of present sects in Christianity, we shall find few that have not in their turns been persecutors, and complainers of persecution. The primitive Christians thought persecution extremely wrong in the Pagans, but practiced it on one another. The first Protestants of the Church of England, blamed persecution in the Roman church, but practiced it against the Puritans... Persecution was therefore not so much the fault of the sect as of the times... The general opinion was only, that those who are in error ought not to persecute the truth: But the possessors of truth were in the right to persecute error, in order to destroy it. Thus, every sect believing itself possessed of all truth... conceived that when the power was in their hands, persecution was a duty required of them by that God whom they supposed to be offended with heresy."[11]

An article, "82. A Bill for Establishing Religious Freedom, 18 June 1779," states,

> "The impious presumption of legislators and rulers, civil as well as ecclesiastical, who, being themselves but fallible and uninspired men, have assumed dominion over the faith of others, setting up their own opinions and modes

of thinking as the only true and infallible, and as such endeavoring to impose them on others, hath established and maintained false religions over the greatest part of the world and through all time: That to compel a man to furnish contributions of money for the propagation of opinions that he disbelieves and abhors, is sinful and tyrannical."[12]

The founding of the early American colonies was an extremely difficult task. An even greater achievement was for those colonies to defy one of the world powers of the eighteenth century to gain total independence. Yet, the greatest task, of monumental difficulty and eternal consequence, began with our founding fathers and continues with us today. How do we survive as a people free from our own government and any foreign government while giving glory to God for our many blessings? We have succeeded, to one degree or another, for 245 years. Yet, America's soul bears old scars and fresh wounds. Let's look at some of the religious persecution that has taken place in our homeland.

- A National Park Service article, "The Massacre of the French," states, "In 1565 . . . when King Philip II of Spain learned that the Frenchman Rene de Laudonniére had established Fort Caroline in Florida, he was incensed - the colony sat on land belonging to the Spanish crown . . . Worst of all to the devoutly Catholic Philip, the settlers were Huguenots (French Protestants) . . . General Pedro Menéndez de Aviles, charged with removing the French . . . led a force to attack Fort Caroline . . . Menéndez was easily able to capture the French settlement, killing most of the men in the battle . . . 111 Frenchmen were killed. Only sixteen were spared including a few who professed being Catholic . . . Two weeks later the sequence of events was repeated . . . This time 134 were killed. From that time, the inlet was called Matanzas - meaning 'slaughters' in Spanish."[13]
- A National Archives article, "Colonization and Settlement (1585–1763)," says, "Spaniards seeking to Christianize the 'New World' and to explore its riches founded the colony of New Mexico in 1598, . . . In 1680, after decades of religious persecution and exploita-

tion by the Spanish, the Pueblos revolted and drove the Spaniards south to El Paso."[14]

- A National Archives article, "Editorial Note," says, "The Province Charter of 1691 provided that there should be 'a liberty of Conscience allowed in the Worship of God to all Christians (Except Papists)' who inhabited Massachusetts. Despite these bold if less than all-embracing words, the faith of the founding Puritans constituted the "establishment" of the province. It continued as such beyond the time of independence and well into the 19th century."[15]

- An article by Samuel W. Rushay, Jr., "Harry Truman's History Lessons," says, "Harry Truman's interest in history is well documented . . . During his lectures at Columbia University on April 29, 1959, former President Truman placed McCarthyism within the broader cycles of 'witch-hunting' and hysteria that he believed had beset the United States since its earliest history. Specific examples included the Salem witch trials of the 1690s."[16]

- A letter "To Thomas Jefferson from Robert Semple, 24 October 1808," says, "The heterogenious union of Church and State, was never congenial to our principles. But when we remember, that from that source, the persecution and imprisonment of many of our ministers arose, we must declare that this union is as repugnant to our feelings, as to our principles."[17]

- A Missouri State Archives document, "The Missouri Mormon War," says, "In 1831 [Joseph] Smith proclaimed that God had designated western Missouri as the place where "Zion" would be "gathered" in anticipation of Christ's second coming. His small band of missionaries soon became a steady stream of converts anxious to establish Zion in Missouri . . . It soon became clear that Missouri non-Mormons and Mormons could not live in the same area harmoniously. In 1836 . . . the state legislature created a new county, 'Caldwell,' in northwest Missouri as a sort of Mormon 'Indian Reservation.' But the booming Mormon population, swelled by the immigration of thousands of eastern converts doomed this to failure. . . In 1838, . . . Missouri's governor, Lilburn Boggs, ordered the Saints expelled from the state, or "exterminated," if necessary . . . On October 30, 1838, an organized mob launched a surprise attack on the small Mormon community of Haun's Mill, massacring eighteen unsuspecting men and boys."[18]

- According to historian Zachary Schrag, writing in *The Encyclopedia of Greater Philadelphia*, "Ethnic and religious antagonism had a long history in the city. Since the 1780s, Irish textile workers had come to Philadelphia after losing their jobs to mechanization in the British Isles. As early as 1828 ... Catholic presence had provoked anxiety among American and Irish-born Protestants ... Anti-Catholic agitation increased in the early 1840s after a Catholic Bishop objected to Protestant teachers' leading students in singing Protestant hymns and requiring them to read from the King James Bible ... In 1844, the Bible controversy intensified when a Catholic school director there suggested suspending Bible reading until the school board could devise a policy acceptable to Catholics and Protestants alike. Nativists saw this as a threat to their liberty ... In May and July 1844, Philadelphia suffered some of the bloodiest rioting of the antebellum period, as anti-immigrant mobs attacked Irish-American homes and Roman Catholic churches before being suppressed by the militia."[19]

Since I was born after World War II ended, I did not experience the horror and anxiety of an attack by foreigners on my homeland, like my Mom and Dad did when Japan attacked Pearl Harbor in 1941. During most of my lifetime, it also seemed as if America had been largely exempted from the persecution and martyrdom for faith in Jesus Christ that I heard about in other countries around the world. I lived my entire life in what I considered to be a relatively safe land, secure from foreign insurgents, until 1993.

- According to a Department of State article, "1993 World Trade Center Bombing," on February 26, 1993, a bomb exploded in the World Trade Center in New York City. Middle Eastern radicals were responsible for the attack.[20]
- A US Government Accountability Office report, "Countering Violent Extremism," says in 1995 the federal building in Oklahoma City was bombed by anti-government far right individuals resulting in 168 lives lost.[21]
- I remember September 11, 2001, like it was yesterday. Islamic radicals hijacked four airplanes. Two of them were flown into the twin towers

of the World Trade Center in New York City. A third plane hit the Pentagon just outside Washington, DC, and the fourth crashed in a field in Pennsylvania. According to the Centers for Disease Control and Prevention, "As of August 16, 2002, a total of 2,726 death certificates related to the WTC attacks have been filed. All but 13 persons died on September 11, 2001."[22] The debilitating effects of those attacks continue today as a variety of respiratory illnesses have been contracted by the emergency workers who responded to help the injured.

- According to the US Extremist Crime Database, since the September 11 attacks, 85 attacks in the United States by violent extremists—associated with both radical Islamist and far-right ideologies—have resulted in 225 fatalities.[23]

These attacks by Islamic extremists and home-grown terrorists were not about land or money. The Islamic extremists hate our faith, freedom, way of life, and proselytizing. The Islamic extremist war on America is based on ideology. However, not all ideological attacks in America are perpetrated by foreigners or Islamists. We have heard reports or watched news coverage of shootings in church services or attacks against Christian groups gathered at schools. These acts were perpetrated by our fellow citizens. The persecution of Christians for their faith has reached American soil. Some of the attacks are instigated by foreign extremists and aided significantly by some of our own countrymen. Sometimes it is an American acting alone against other Americans. But make no mistake. This war is against the truth, and Satan is behind every attack, prompting, goading, and inciting misguided or ungodly people to achieve his goals.

The devil is a master strategist at spiritual warfare. He has engaged in a war of attrition for thousands of years. He wants to rob God of glory by inflicting as much damage as possible on the Body of Christ. The devil is engaged in an all-out spiritual war against anyone who loves Jesus or anyone who is considering giving their life to Christ. Wounded Christians may be less likely to praise God, present a Christlike witness, or evangelize; compared to when they are healthy. Lucifer's plan of attack is to wound every Christian until they become completely ineffective or, hopefully, renounce their faith. He has targeted several specific groups or types of believers within each local body of Christ for continual harassment, those through whom the Holy Spirit is accomplishing great things for the kingdom of heaven and the leaders of each local body of Christ, who are diligently serving under the Spirit's guidance. We need to pray for, encourage, and assist these kingdom workers in every way possible. They are equipping us, building us up, preparing us for good works in the kingdom, and praying for us. We need to ensure they understand we appreciate what they do for us and that we want to help them do the same for others.

Chapter 11

The State of the Union

> For although they knew God, they neither glorified him as God nor gave thanks to him, but their thinking became futile and their foolish hearts were darkened . . . Furthermore, just as they did not think it worthwhile to retain the knowledge of God, so God gave them over to a depraved mind, so that they do what ought not to be done. (Romans 1:21, 28)

I love America, and I always have. After living in a foreign country for two years, I came to appreciate and love America even more, particularly the freedoms we enjoy. I feel privileged to have been born and raised in the United States. God has blessed our country mightily in our short history. However, I don't believe God will continue to do so if we, as a nation, continue to separate ourselves from him. I realize if I'm looking for a country in great spiritual need, where I could be assigned as an ambassador for the kingdom of heaven, I need look no further than my own town, state, and country. America is in deep spiritual trouble, and it is getting worse with each passing year. This condition is not hard to recognize. Let's review a few of the symptoms, which are by no means all-inclusive.

- American expenditures for prescription medications increased from $205 billion in 2005 to over $334 billion in 2017.[1]

- In 2017, 4.5 percent of US adults (eleven million) and 9.4 percent of US adolescents ages 12 to 17 (2.3 million) suffered from at least one major depressive episode with severe impairment of major life activities.[2]
- Deaths by suicide per 100,000 persons increased from 10.1 in 1999 to 14.3 in 2018.[3]
- According to a National Institute of Mental Health article, suicide was the tenth leading cause of death in the United States in 2016, claiming the lives of nearly forty-five thousand people. Among Americans ages ten to thirty-four, suicide was the second leading cause of death.[4]

The Centers for Disease Control and Prevention has reported the following.

- "Nearly 45,000 lives were lost to suicide in 2016. Suicide rates went up more than 30% in half of states since 1999. More than half of people who died by suicide did not have a known mental health condition."[5]
- A database titled "PMR Query System for Occupation" provides several significant points regarding a study of suicides by profession in twenty-six states from 1999–2014. It notes clergy is not immune to suicide. The clergy profession has a lower suicide rate than the average suicide rate in other professions in the United States, but clergy are still at risk, particularly Black male clergy and White female clergy. The "proportionate mortality ratio" of Black male clergy and White female clergy were 21 percent higher and 6 percent higher, respectively, than the average proportionate suicide rate in other professions.[6]
- "An analysis of 2016 U.S. drug overdose data shows that America's overdose epidemic is spreading geographically and increasing across demographic groups . . . Drug overdoses killed 63,632 Americans in 2016."[7]
- More than seventy-two thousand Americans died from drug overdoses in 2017. The death of Americans from drug overdoses more than tripled from 2002 to 2017.[8]

Now, add some of the societal changes enumerated earlier.

- The family unit is disintegrating.
- Sanctity of life, particularly related to the unborn, is eroding further.
- We are experiencing a significant increase in random mass violence.

Just for good measure, consider the degradation of the Word of God within the Body of Christ already mentioned.

- Forty-one percent of Christians say knowing what is right or wrong is a matter of personal experience. This view is much more prevalent among younger generations than among older adults.
- Fifty-nine percent of Christians believe moral truth is absolute.[9]

As a Christian, does my personal experience replace the Word of God regarding what is right and wrong in the eyes of God? No! This is diametrically opposed to what Scripture teaches us. The last two points show an alarming pattern of relativism replacing the truth within a significant portion of the Body of Christ. The picture painted by the facts is revealing. They give us a clear indication for many people in America: these days are dark spiritually speaking. These facts are not designed to be a scare tactic but a reality check.

Each day is important because it is the last opportunity for salvation for many of our fellow citizens. In 2019, the National Vital Statistics System recorded over 2.8 million deaths in America.[10] That's an average of 7,821 deaths per day, 325 per hour, and over 5 per minute. How many of those deaths occurred in my community? I don't know. How many of those people died without Jesus Christ as their Lord and Savior? I don't know. Regardless of the actual number, each one saddens Jesus.

Is there reason for concern regarding the spiritual life of Americans as a whole? In October 2019, the Pew Research Center released an article entitled, "In U.S., Decline of Christianity Continues at Rapid Pace." The title summarizes the findings of their study in 2018–2019 compared with a similar study done in 2009. The survey taken in 2018–2019 revealed the following.

65% of American adults describe themselves as Christians . . . down 12 percentage points over the past decade . . . [The percentage of] people who describe their religious identity as atheist, agnostic or "nothing in particular," now stands at 26%, up from 17% in 2009 . . . 43% of U.S. adults identify with

Protestantism, down from 51% in 2009 . . . More than eight-in-ten members of the Silent Generation (those born between 1928 and 1945) describe themselves as Christians (84%), as do three-quarters of Baby Boomers (76%). In stark contrast, 49% of Millennials describe themselves as Christians . . . and 64% of Millennials attend worship services a few times a year or less.[11]

In December 2011, the Pew Research Center released an article entitled, "Global Christianity—A Report on the Size and Distribution of the World's Christian Population," which stated,

There are 2.18 billion Christians of all ages around the world, representing nearly a third of the estimated 2010 global population of 6.9 billion . . . Christians make up about the same portion of the world's population today (32%) as they did a century ago (35%) . . . Although Europe and the Americas still are home to a majority of the world's Christians (63%), that share is much lower than it was in 1910 (93%) . . . At the same time . . . the share of the population that is Christian in sub-Saharan Africa climbed from 9% in 1910 to 63% in 2010, while in the Asia-Pacific region it rose from 3% to 7%.[12]

It appears the percentage of Christians in the population worldwide is not decreasing but is shifting from the Americas and Europe to Africa and Asia.

Some opposed to Christ have eagerly proclaimed the death knell of Christianity in America and around the world. Whether Christianity is declining in America or not, it appears to be holding steady worldwide and increasing significantly in some areas outside the United States, where Christianity is brutally oppressed. God is not concerned only with the souls in America but with every soul on the planet. Those who know Jesus also know his body of believers on earth will never be eradicated. Nothing can prevail against the kingdom of heaven. Furthermore, I am convinced God wants to continue to draw those who are earnestly seeking the truth. He wants to accomplish this through those who love him and his Son because we are his preferred tool for proclaiming the gospel message.

Chapter 12

The Opportunity is Today

> Be very careful, then, how you live—not as unwise but as wise, making the most of every opportunity, because the days are evil. (Ephesians 5:15–16)

Those who believe in Jesus Christ as Lord and Savior can navigate these turbulent waters through the Holy Spirit's guidance. The Spirit will carry us through the worldly dangers to the eternal shore of heaven. Jesus promised that nothing will prevail against his Church (Matthew 16:18). Such is not the case for the unsaved. They are in dire straits, to use a mariner's term. I know the previous pages may have painted a picture of gloom and doom for some, but my objective is not to cause believers to feel despondent or helpless. My goal is to make believers fully aware of the source of changes taking place in America and highlight the tremendous opportunity before us. Whether we are ruled by a democratic government or some other form of government is not the most important point. Democracy in the United States will end either when the Lord returns or before. Scripture guarantees Christians will be persecuted for their faith. This fact should become clearer each day for believers in our homeland. The most important question for Christians is, will we continue to stand firm in the faith, regardless of circumstances? In his book *The Gathering Storm*, Dr. Albert Mohler says, "There is no external threat—even in a secular age—that can truly threaten the gospel of Christ, nor the eternal promises that Christ has made to his church . . . Not even death will truly threaten the promises of God in the gospel of Christ. The great threat we face is not to the church's existence, but to its faithfulness."[1] We need to view every day the Lord gives us as a gift to be used to present the gospel message to the lost. We must understand the urgency of utilizing today as efficiently and effectively as possible.

I am convinced the gift of time is second only to God's gift of grace through the sacrifice of his Son, Jesus Christ. I have a friend who likes to tell me, "I woke up on the right side of the grass this morning. The rest is gravy." He means it, and I appreciate his godly attitude on the matter of time. I have already spoken of a "second chance philosophy" or an attitude of "there's always tomorrow" toward life. Those attitudes are extravagances that we cannot afford. However, we also need to be careful not to make fundamental mistakes in our zeal to do something. In my human mindset, I have decided if I truly appreciate the gift of time, I should do something significant for the kingdom of heaven today. Such thinking is flawed from the very start. I have decided that I should do something. Wrong! I should not be deciding. I should be seeking what God has planned for me to do. I need to listen expectantly for his Spirit to lead me wherever I am supposed to go and allow him to work through me as he sees fit. The Holy Spirit is the originator of the spiritual power. I am only the conductor of his power. I need to concentrate on building a more intimate relationship with God, and everything else will fall into place.

Oswald Chambers summed up this matter of "doing" compared to "relationship" very well. He wrote in his book, *My Utmost for His Highest*, "It is arduous work to keep the master ambition in front. It means holding one's self to the high ideal year in and year out, not being ambitious to win souls or to establish churches or to have revivals, but being ambitious only to be 'accepted of Him'."[2]

It's not about me. It's not about doing something for the kingdom in the name of Jesus. It's all about a relationship with God and his Son Jesus. Then the Holy Spirit will use me appropriately for his kingdom purposes.

I am still working on prioritizing relationships above "doing," though I have not yet wholly incorporated this discipline into my spiritual life. When I think about my most important human relationships and those who were most influential in my decision to accept Jesus Christ as Lord and Savior, I draw three conclusions.

- Many of these people were a generation or more older than me.

- All these people desired to have an intimate relationship with me.
- All these people cared about my well-being here on earth and eternally.

Each of these people decided to spend a significant amount of time with me. My immediate family was stuck with me. It was their "job" to provide for me. They didn't have to nurture and love me, but they did, and not because of anything I had done for them. They loved and cared for me because I was part of their family. Those outside my family had no legal responsibility for me whatsoever. Yet, each of these people made it a priority to get to know me intimately. Their words carried great weight with me because I knew they loved me, and they wanted what was best for me. When it comes to relationships, this old cliché is so true: "No one cares how much you know until they know how much you care." I know this to be true from personal experience. You probably do too.

Relationships can be tricky to establish and even harder to maintain. They need regular evaluation and recalibration to stay on an even keel. What started as a great relationship may not always remain so and vice versa. My friend Mike once gave me straightforward advice on this matter. He said, "You need to regularly evaluate your relationships. Every relationship you have either draws you closer to or pushes you further from Christ. Those that push you away from Christ need to be corrected or abandoned." Of course, Mike was not including marital relationships in that advice. Relationships are crucial, as difficult as they may be sometimes. The kingdom of heaven is about two relationships, one eternal and one temporal: our relationship with God Almighty through his Son Jesus Christ and our relationship with our fellow people.

Building Relationships in Heaven

God's Word places our love of him and relationship to him as the most important calling in our lives. Scripture also tells us Jesus, who has seen God and is in closest relationship with God, has made God known to us (John 1:18). Since Jesus Christ is our perfect example of how we should live, we should desire to be in close relationship with God as well. My human inclination is to "prove" my love for God by doing good things, by bearing fruit, but Jesus told us, "Seek first his kingdom and his righteousness and everything else we need will be provided to us as well (Matthew 6:33).

Oswald Chambers had much to say regarding relationship to God compared with doing things for God. Three of the nuggets he wrote on this topic in his book, *My Utmost for His Highest*, include:

- "'Take no thought for your life. Be careful about one thing only' says our Lord, 'your relationship to Me'."[3]
- "Jesus Christ says, in effect, Don't rejoice in successful service, but rejoice because you are rightly related to me . . . It is the work that God does through us that counts, not what we do for Him. All that Our Lord heeds in a man's life is the relationship of worth to His Father."[4]
- Our Lord never dictated to His Father, and we are not here to dictate to God; we are here to submit to His will so that He may work through us what He wants.[5]

Just as God is patient in waiting for lost souls to accept Jesus Christ as Lord and Savior, he is also waiting patiently for every believer to approach him, wanting them to build a deeper relationship with him. But God doesn't always wait. He pursues Christians on occasion to initiate or intensify relationship building.

Susie and I love vacations at the beach. Two of the last three summers of Dad's life, he went with us. Those vacations were even more memorable for me because he was there. One vacation stands out above all the others. In 2013, we had the opportunity to spend two weeks in a penthouse condo on the twentieth floor overlooking the Gulf of Mexico. The balcony off the living room faced due west with an amazing panoramic view. We checked into the condo on Saturday afternoon. On Saturday evening we were, as usual, sitting on the balcony near sunset watching the waves, and God did not disappoint. There were no clouds on the horizon, and we had an unobstructed view of a spectacular sunset. Our vacation had gotten off to a perfect start, but the best was yet to come.

The next day, on Sunday evening, shortly before sunset I had not yet gone onto the balcony. I heard a faint noise in the condo but couldn't figure out the source. Finally, I realized it had to be coming from outside the building. I walked onto the balcony and saw a lone figure standing on the beach near the water. No one was around him. The man was dressed in full Scottish regalia from head to toe, complete with Balmoral hat, kilt, and knee-high socks with tasseled garters. I listened as he played "Amazing Grace" and "America the Beautiful" on his bagpipes as the sun lowered, and then disappeared into the ocean. The Lord had come to visit with me in a very special way. It was a brief, magnificent worship service unlike any I have experienced in a church building. I was moved in a profound way by such a gracious gift. I never saw or heard the Scotsman again. The Lord reminded me he is with me every day, in the church building, at work, or at the beach. The manner of his visit was totally unexpected but very much appreciated. The God of all creation came to me and met me where I was, just to spend time with me. He has always been willing to meet me where I am. I'm convinced that just as God provided me with a "special time," he will also provide me with opportunities to spend special time with others on his behalf.

Dad told me the Lord spoke to him audibly one time. As Dad was driving home alone one evening, the Lord told him to go visit a longtime friend immediately. Dad told the Lord he was very tired and would go in the morning to see his friend. Early the next morning, Dad drove to his friend's house and was told his friend had died just a few hours earlier. Dad didn't even know his friend was sick. Dad said the Lord never spoke to him audibly again. We need to be prepared whenever the Lord presents us with an invitation to do his will. If we are unprepared for the opportunity and miss it, a second chance is never guaranteed.

The simple truth is, God wants to have an intimate relationship with me. God saw my body before it was even formed. He adopted me as a son, placed his Spirit within me, and gave me the right to call him Father. He wants me to love him and learn everything about him I am able. The same is true of you. God works most effectively through those who have grown into an intimate relationship with him and are willing to fully surrender their lives to him.

Building Relationships Outside the Body of Christ

God has called us to take the message of the kingdom of heaven to all people. How, then, can we possibly communicate the truth to lost souls without alienating them? It sounds difficult doesn't it? But really, it isn't. The Holy Spirit is working worldwide, every minute of every day, wooing lost souls, and convicting them of their sins. Some of those whom the Spirit pursues will harden their hearts. Others will open their hearts to the gospel message. Those who are open to God's calling are the "field ripe for harvest." It is this field I am seeking. These are the people who, like the Ethiopian eunuch, want someone like Philip to talk with them about these matters and answer their questions. Some of those questions may be unpleasant, dealing with the evil nature of humans and eternal torment, but the focus will be God's love for every one of us. Every human needs God's forgiveness through Jesus Christ. So, we wait for sincere inquiries from those who are lost and then respond scripturally, lovingly, and with humility.

In their book, *Unchristian*, David Kinnaman and Gabe Lyons say, "When we asked born-again Busters (aged twenty-six to forty-four in 2010) to identify the activity, ministry event, or person most directly responsible for their decision to accept Jesus Christ, seventy one percent listed an individual—typically their parent, a friend, another relative, or a teacher."[6]

I am convinced many people in America are searching for the truth. These people are open to at least consider the gospel message. I look for people who have a desire to talk with me. I try to let them lead the conversation to see if they are interested in spiritual matters. (Sometimes I jump in too soon with what I think, but I'm getting better at waiting.) My hope is to meet someone who has a desire to learn who Jesus Christ is and what he has done for me. In my personal testimony, I have no desire to tell listeners what they need (unless they ask me directly). I tell them why I needed Jesus Christ, how I found Jesus Christ, what I believe about eternity, and what Jesus Christ has done for me since I accepted him as Lord and Savior.

If they are interested in hearing additional details, I tell them I was separated from God because of my sins and how sick and tired I was of living with guilt and shame. I also tell them about the joy, peace, and sense of purpose I have now. If I present my testimony in the first person, what I needed, and what Jesus Christ did for me, and I make no comments about what the listener needs, they don't feel obligated to respond. The conversation is "safe" for them. My testimony is about me, not them. In silence, they can choose to accept or reject my opinions. If, after I tell someone my story, they say "goodbye" and walk away, so be it. I will have done the best I know how to do. If, and only if, the listener so desires, they can carry the conversation about the matter further, and I gladly answer any questions I can. I am convinced the Holy Spirit takes over at this point. The Spirit knows perfectly if a listener is seeking the truth. If so, he will speak through me, telling the lost soul exactly what he or she needs to hear.

Usually, such a conversation does not occur the first time you meet an unsaved person. Normally, you meet a person with whom you have some common interest and, if you like each other, you get together more as time passes. Hopefully, this person will see something different about you. After all, joy and peace are not plentiful in this world. Sometimes we forget that people who weren't raised attending worship services may be very uncomfortable in a church setting. Jesus went to meet the people where they were: on the hillside, the seashore, and in the streets. He spoke to large gatherings of people and then spent one-on-one time with individuals who were interested in his message. We need to meet the lost where they are too. Most of us are surrounded by them every day.

Kari, a dear sister in Christ, had been witnessing for some time to a coworker who was a babe in Christ. For some reason this coworker became jealous of Kari. When attempts to resolve this contention failed, Kari was prepared to resign her position and seek employment elsewhere rather than risk damaging her witness. When the coworker found out Kari was going to leave the company, she talked to Kari about it, and their relationship was restored. Kari said she kept reminding herself why she was at work: to spread the good news of Jesus Christ. Kari understood God didn't place her with this employer just so she could provide for her family. God placed her there to minister. I was humbled by Kari's focus on the primary purpose of her employment. This was also the first time I heard of someone who was willing to give up a job to protect her witness to another person.

Like Kari, we have all been called to be God's ambassadors, spreading the ministry of reconciliation everywhere we go. Jesus spent time building relationships with those who wanted to get to know him. Likewise, we need to develop relationships, beginning at home. We should also be intentional about building relationships in the other place we spend most of our time: at work. It seems like a natural place to minister. We spend many hours with our coworkers and get to know them quite well. If we remember that each step we take in life is a journey with Jesus Christ at our side, our experience at work can take on a whole new meaning. We will be more apt to look for opportunities to witness. Suddenly, a day at the office can be exciting and joyful as we anticipate what may lie ahead. If we don't view our place of employment as a potential field ripe for the harvest, we are destined to miss some opportunities.

I understand the value of a Christian building a personal relationship with a lost soul because it was instrumental in my conversion. Bob and Gary were two Christians I mentioned earlier. I met them while attending a small church in Dayton, Ohio. They showed me they wanted to be friends, if I was willing. Neither seemed to be in a hurry to convince me of my need for Jesus Christ, though I was, in fact, in great need. They were content to simply spend time with me, so we could get to know each other. Over time we became good friends. As we spent time together, they shared some of the ways the Lord had helped and blessed them. They planted the seeds, watered them, and waited for God's Spirit to convict me. My wife, Susie, Bob, Sue, Gary, and Cindy were some of the most influential believers who helped lead me back to Jesus Christ. Even with the Spirit's help, it took time, which they willingly gave.

I am extraordinarily grateful that God called me to be his own. The manner of my conversion is quite ordinary. What the Holy Spirit did for me, he has done for millions of others through the centuries. Mine is a common human story, repeated since Jesus Christ first asked twelve men to follow him. It is the one-on-one interaction, the caring and sharing from one person to another, where we can best show the love of Jesus Christ to the world. Think about it! What person or persons were the most influential in your decision to give your life to the Lord? How did they affect your decision? You don't have to look very far to see numerous examples of souls led to Christ by a single person, or a few persons, who started out being a friend.

Building Relationships Within the Body of Christ

The universal Body of Christ is the worldwide group of people who are called by God and have accepted Jesus as Lord and Savior. Unity in faith and purpose are two of the foundational characteristics of this body. On the night of his arrest, Jesus prayed the believers would be one, just as Jesus and the Father are one. The early church devoted themselves to the apostles' teaching, fellowship, the breaking of bread, and prayer. The apostles performed many signs and wonders, and all the believers had everything in common. As a result, the Lord added to their number daily. This oneness in faith and purpose we see in the first-century church does not seem to be as predominant today. My experience is, the unity in the Body of Christ is eroding. Having spent more than thirty years in church, I've had plenty of opportunities to observe how the local body of Christ interacts with each other and with those outside the body. As a Christian, I hoped the local body of Christ would be just like those people who helped lead me to Christ. I hoped almost every Christian would be dedicated to leading lost souls to Christ and then helping those souls become mature disciples of the Lord. Maybe I was expecting too much.

It would be interesting to know the percentage of people in America who regularly attend worship services but have little or no other contact with the local body of Christ. I would also like to know what percentage of regular church attendees volunteer for service projects and ministries outside the church building. I've heard it said more than once, "Twenty percent of the congregation does eighty percent of the ministerial work here." I don't know who first made this statement or if those numbers are correct. If the statement is true, such a situation seems contrary to God's design. He created us with a deep-seated desire to form intimate, lasting friendships and has called us to develop those relationships while working together to further the kingdom of heaven.

Our church body had a picnic each summer, designed to introduce ourselves to the community in a "non-preachy," family-oriented way. This outreach required many volunteers, but did not require any special skills. In 1996 I had the opportunity to join Mike, Kim, Jackie, Gary, Penny, Bill, and Marsha in a one-week service trip to Grenada to engage in construction work on a church building. While I was involved in prison ministry in Louisville, numerous individuals volunteered to help lead singing or give their testimony in worship services held at the correctional facility. These are just three opportunities I had to serve God and people while getting to know my fellow brothers and sisters in Christ much more intimately. These times produced an instant connection, a lasting bond between other believers and me that will have a positive impact on the remainder of my life.

Worship and service have a common thread. Worship is proclaiming value, giving worth and praise to God the Father and his Son, Jesus Christ. Service is also assigning value, giving worth to the person or persons we are serving in the name of Jesus Christ. By serving, we give value to those we serve, showing them they are important to us, just like Jesus did as he served people. In worship and service, those worshipping and serving are voluntarily placing themselves under someone else to bring glory to God. As we grow in love with each other, we grow in love with God.

New Christians need like-minded friends to help them flourish. They need mature believers to model Christian living and selfless service for the kingdom of heaven. I was fortunate. Bob and Sue continued to spend time with Susie and me after my conversion. They were great models for Christian living and provided a continual source of encouragement as I was learning to walk with Christ. Sue, Bob's wife, is a very relational person. She loves people, and one of the ways she expresses her love is with hugs. I still remember the first time Sue told me, "A hug is a paycheck of the heart." I'm rich because of all the "paychecks" she has given me. A small plaque, given to me by Bob and Sue says, "God said it. I believe it. That settles it." We could even shorten the motto if we wanted. "God said it. That settles it." Truth is truth whether we believe it or not. Here is one certain truth: godly friendship is a treasure beyond measure.

The time we spend with Christians in small groups, social settings, and ministry activities is beneficial to us all. Through these interactions we encourage and assist each other and grow in our walk with the Lord. As we spend more time with saved souls, we begin to identify each other's spiritual gifts and passions. This is very useful information, particularly if I am looking for believers who may have spiritual gifts and desires beneficial to the ministry of my heart. I believe God shaped me to serve in prison ministry. In a local body of Christ, I don't think you usually find many Christians who say prison ministry is their calling, and understandably so. I'm always looking for someone who may be willing to join me in that ministry. God is perfectly faithful. He will bring partners to help strengthen and grow the ministry where he has placed you, for his glory.

The Body of Christ—All Parts Required

In addition to unity in faith and purpose, another foundational characteristic of the Body of Christ is that every single part is indispensable. It was God who placed each part in the body, by his design, desiring all parts of the body to have equal concern for each other. Young or old in age, new or mature in the faith, having different spiritual gifts, all are a part of the Body of Christ by God's plan. He designed us to work together to achieve the purposes he designed for us. Every Christian has his or her own individual life to lead. As we go through life on our own, we should take advantage of every opportunity to point others to Jesus Christ. However, God did not create us to live our spiritual lives on our own. If I think I can do everything alone, I am deluded.

When I was a youngster in church older Christians complained about the style of music and not being valued by the church as a whole. Some older Christians are complaining about the same things today. Each group is committed to the validity of their position on this topic. I am also convinced both sides contribute to this problem as well.

Dan and Meg are two dear friends, who serve as missionaries far from America. They have served in several places where Christians must deal with significant persecution for their faith. One day as Dan and I sat in a school gymnasium watching our grandchildren play basketball, he made an interesting observation: "The Christians living in places where persecution exists don't argue about the small stuff, like the style of music. They have real issues. They're just happy they get to worship God." All believers in America would do well to reflect on the religious freedom we enjoy, a fact we may very well take for granted. An easy life can breed complacency. The point is, the body of Christ in America should focus on eliminating division over non-essential matters and promote unity as much as possible. God wants the entire Body of Christ to love, nurture, and encourage each other, pooling their gifts to achieve the greatest good for the kingdom of heaven.

I have seen brothers and sisters in Christ with decades of experience in Christian living who have either chosen or accepted the role of spectator within the Body of Christ. Sometimes this is a willful choice by a particular Christian, possibly because the person feels he or she has done enough for the Body of Christ and is at the age the person can "retire" from Christian service. Sometimes a Christian believes or assumes their local body does not desire their services any longer. How tragic it is to see an experienced believer, ready and willing to serve, relegated to the role of observer, no matter the reason. Our mature men and women in the faith should be honored for their longstanding devotion to Christ and utilized by the local body of Christ because they have so much experience and wisdom to offer. The Bible tells us, "Stand up in the presence of the aged, show respect for the elderly" (Leviticus 19:32) and to treat older men as fathers and older women as mothers (1 Timothy 5:1–2).

If a Christian assumes he or she is irrelevant or unwanted, the person will be prone to withdraw from or lessen their participation within the Body of Christ and stagnate. Every saved soul is vital to the Body of Christ, bringing special characteristics and gifts just as God orchestrated. Generally speaking, younger Christians bring an exuberance, a vitality, and an energy that is difficult for the senior group to match. The younger group, simply by their age and common interests, also brings a built-in connection to the younger generation of lost souls. The older Christians bring extensive experience in living a life for Christ, along with patience and maturity, commodities less prevalent in the younger group.

God's Word contains instructions for the Body of Christ, some common to both groups and some differing instructions, specific to each group. Each group has a responsibility to the other as well as to lost souls. For example, younger believers have a responsibility to honor senior Christians and learn from the elders' experiences. Mature believers have a responsibility to teach believers by setting a Christlike example and working with younger Christians to develop their skills. Each group is commanded to work together in unity and love to portray Jesus Christ to the world. When younger believers combine their strength, energy, and exuberance with older Christians' experience and wisdom, the local body of Christ can minister efficiently and effectively for the kingdom of heaven as the faith of every ministering believer is bolstered.

Dad knew a man who raised and trained bluetick hounds. As the dog owner explained, the only things required of him for the pups to be trained were time and patience. The seasoned hound dog would do the training. The dog owner would take the pups out with a seasoned hound to hunt. The pups would watch the older hound hunt his quarry, following his every move. Over time, through imitation, the pups would learn what to do from the seasoned dog. Then the dog owner would take the pup out to hunt without the seasoned veteran. Things work the same way in the human world. Our mothers, fathers, and other adults taught us and we teach our children. Spiritually speaking, the Holy Spirit, utilizing Scripture, teaches maturing believers who, in turn, teach younger Christians. Every single part of the Body of Christ has a critical function. God designed it this way.

Have you seen groups or individuals in your local congregation who have withdrawn or stagnated? I hope not. Satan is the only winner in such a situation. The Body of Christ has never had the luxury of allowing willing servants, young or old, to sit idly on the sidelines. The Spirit of God did not develop people from "babes in Christ" to mature believers so they could become observers. Each day we move one day closer to eternity. With each new day, we have one less day to help saved souls grow or point lost souls toward Christ.

Another foundational characteristic about the Body of Christ is that the Lord's love always produces godly action in those who love him. Christ's love, as Paul said, compels me to respond to the world with godly action as well (1 Corinthians 5:14–15). I rarely, if ever, do this perfectly. Many times, I don't do it well. Sometimes I fail to do it at all, but I do keep trying. One thing God's love has communicated to me is that he has a plan for my life. He has specific things he wants me to accomplish for his kingdom if I am willing.

We all need somebody to give us a helping hand through life. I had Mom, Dad, Susie, Bob, Sue, Gary, Cindy, Mike, Suzy, Rick, Kari, and many others. David had Jonathan. Elisha had Elijah. Naomi had Ruth. Timothy had Paul.

Who has you?

Prioritizing Time

We all make time for the things most important to us. Some of these priorities are premeditated decisions while others are formed internally, with little or no conscious thought. (We don't have to set an alarm clock to know when it's time for our next meal.) Regardless of how priorities are set, one priority will usually take precedence in our lives. The number-one priority speaks volumes about our spiritual well-being because it is our god, so to speak. How often do we really consider the eternal ramifications of the priorities we set here on earth?

Most of us need to make money to buy food, clothes, and put a roof over our heads, but how much is enough when it comes to money? One of the ways our sinful nature has manifested itself throughout history is in the form of idol worship. Back in the Old Testament times, people worshipped manmade idols such as a golden calf or an Asherah pole. In America the calf and the pole have been replaced by other idols, such as wealth, fame, sex, and power. We have all known or met an individual whose life was consumed, or at least dominated, by a single goal. If the goal is not bringing glory and honor to God, or if the goal is placed above God, serious spiritual problems arise.

I've known several persons who suffered from a common obsession: climbing the corporate ladder to attain a position of power or fame. These workaholics could be found at the office at any given time. God, family, and everything else played second, third, or fourth fiddle to the company. Even family time was used to schedule events for the benefit of conducting business or strengthening business ties. The need for power can be as intoxicating as any drug. This obsession will eventually absorb all of a person's time, to the exclusion of everything else.

I remember attending a business meeting being addressed by a high-level executive. As he recounted his career path with the firm, he stated, proud as a peacock, that he had gone through three wives for the sake of his career. The only thing he bemoaned was the financial cost of those three divorces. It has always been my hope that career would never rise above fourth on my list of priorities. God first, my wife second, the rest of my family third, and then maybe work.

Another time-consuming obsession is the accumulation of wealth. America, at least statistically, is among the world leaders in this endeavor, ranking either first or second on every published list of countries with the most billionaires. Some may say this focus on wealth only applies to a few (the billionaires) in our country, but evidence indicates average Americans have an unhealthy preoccupation with accumulating and maintaining "stuff" even if we don't use it. Consider the self-storage industry in our country. It has no equal on the face of the earth. I am not innocent in this matter. While I have never rented a storage unit, I have always owned a house with a basement and an outbuilding where I have stored stuff that I haven't used for years. Aren't there others who could put those things to good use? When is enough, enough? Scripture gives us a clear answer. Whoever loves money never has enough. Whoever loves wealth is never satisfied with their income (Ecclesiastes 5:10). Wealth panders to greed, a powerful, sinful drive within us. If we allow greed to take hold, it will consume us.

On the other end of the "accumulating wealth" spectrum is a small group who renounce all the trappings of the world while dedicating their lives to the Lord's service. Mother Teresa is one example. These are two extremes regarding the accumulation of wealth. Most of us fall somewhere in between. I am not suggesting any or all of us should quit our jobs and move to Asia or Africa to teach the good news to the lost—unless God has called you to such a mission. What I am advocating is that we seize every opportunity wherever we are to start building relationships with lost souls so, in time, they may have a desire to be introduced to Jesus Christ. Everywhere you go, the church building, work, the PTA meeting, your child's ballgame, and the grocery store, people are there for you to meet, some who know the Lord and some who don't. Those who know the Lord need your encouragement and companionship to reach their potential, as you need theirs. Those who don't know the Lord need your witness to introduce them to the Savior.

The bottom line is, we are responsible for how we manage our time. We decide when, where, and how we are going to spend our time. We need to identify those important and urgent things, as Dwight Eisenhower laid out in his decision matrix. Then we prioritize the order for accomplishing these things. Our value systems dictate what is important and urgent. Those who claim Jesus Christ as Lord and Savior have achieved the most important goal in our lives: eternal life with Christ. How then are we, as Christians, called to utilize our time? Scripture emphasizes building our relationship with the Father, the saved, and the unsaved (which pretty much covers everybody). It is not the "who" but the "what." Scripture emphasizes relationships, showing us that all these relationships are important and urgent. Regardless of who we are engaging, building these relationships takes time, a precious commodity that many don't want to give. Jesus's example to us is the exact opposite. He lived with those he was mentoring.

The importance of relationships in ministry cannot be overstated. Let's look at the example of Jesus, who was the very best at building personal relationships. In his book, *They Smell Like Sheep*, Lynn Anderson says, "Of the three biblical models, shepherd, mentor, and equipper, the chief model is that of shepherd—and with good reason, for a shepherd is someone who lives with sheep. A shepherd knows each sheep by name; he nurtures the young, bandages the wounded, cares for the weak, and protects them all. A shepherd smells like sheep."[7] Lynn continues: "Shepherding sheep requires a long-term, costly commitment of self, time, and energy and the building of open, authentic relationships."[8]

Jesus Christ spent most of his time with twelve men and a number of women as he prepared them to carry on his ministry. He poured his life into these people before he poured out his life on the cross. Every one of us has experienced the time-consuming, painstaking effort required to develop relationships with people. It doesn't happen overnight. In fact, the building of a particular relationship continues throughout the existence of the relationship. It never ends. Jesus showed us that the power of our witness comes from relationship. He formed relationships, so people could get to know him intimately. Then they would understand who he is. Likewise, we need the power of relationships for our witness to be effective. Shortcuts don't exist.

Our lives on earth are short. We are dying, and so is our world. Remembering these facts will help us keep our priorities in the proper eternal perspective. My younger brother, Tim, provided me with a tangible reminder of the importance of prioritizing time. After he accepted Jesus Christ as Lord and Savior, Tim taped a saying to the doorframe in his bedroom next to the light switch. He placed it there so he would see it each time he left the bedroom. It read, "Live today as you will wish you had lived it come judgment day." Sage advice for all believers.

Transparency

Vulnerability is another unpopular aspect of relationship building. Everyone has struggles and flaws. As we spend more time with someone, the imperfections in each person become more apparent. It is possible a person may become disillusioned with me as they realize my flaws because they initially thought I was a "good person" or a "good Christian." It is also possible that someone may decide he or she doesn't want to continue spending time with me when the person realizes these defects. When we try to establish an intimate relationship, we always risk rejection, but if we can't show our true selves, we can't ever achieve real intimacy. I am convinced time and possible rejection are two major stumbling blocks to building relationships. Jesus knew far in advance that he would be rejected by most people, yet he did reveal himself, undeterred. When Jesus of Nazareth revealed himself, he was rejected by his own brothers, by his hometown, and by religiously educated Jews who should have known who he was.

Unlike Jesus, we are sinful people with a sinful nature. As I start to develop a relationship with someone, they will soon notice I exhibit characteristics unlike Christ, even though I am a professing Christian. Believers should understand this contradiction, since we know we are saved but still sinful and far from perfect. However, this contradiction may be confusing for those who do not understand Scripture. In such cases, it is important for me to proclaim Jesus Christ, my Lord and Savior, as the only sinless human ever to walk this earth and admit my weakness and my sinfulness as well as my desire to become more like Christ, though it will be in an imperfect way. Those who would use me as a measure of what Christians are supposed to look like must be pointed to Jesus Christ, the perfect example of how believers are supposed to live.

Speaking the Truth in Love

The truth can be a harsh reality. Consider the following.

- The nature of humans is evil.
- The sinful nature of humans is present from conception.
- Everything that does not come from faith is sin.
- The penalty of sin is death.

If we don't understand and accept these statements as truth, we will never realize our need for salvation. Christians have come to understand these hard facts on their journey to the foot of the cross. Conveying the truth to lost souls needs to be handled deftly. Scripture tells us the world hated Jesus because he testified the works of the world are evil (John 7:7) and that the world will hate believers because of Jesus (Mark 13:13).

However, not everyone will hate our message. Every generation has souls who, through the Holy Spirit's prompting, are seeking the truth. They are lost souls, under conviction, just like we were before conversion. For some of those lost souls, we are the mouthpieces God intends to use, if we are willing to engage them and tell them the truth in love. Lost souls must come to the realization that they are separated from God by sin and in need of a Savior before they can repent and be saved. However, the foundational message of the gospel we are to proclaim is "good news;" a message of love, hope, and redemption. Consider the following:

- God wants everyone to come to repentance.
- God loves us so much that he sent his Son to die for our sins.
- The gift of God is eternal life in Christ Jesus our Lord.

We are called to present the message of grace to lost souls. Every lost soul who learns of God's holiness and the sacrifice of his sinless Son will also understand that we, as humans, cannot compare to such a standard. If an unsaved person's concerns turn to the topic of unworthiness or eternal separation from God during a conversation, we should be prepared to address those topics with confidence because God's love expressed through Jesus's sacrifice is the remedy for every human flaw.

THE OPPORTUNITY IS TODAY

The advances of technology I have witnessed in my lifetime are nothing short of amazing.

- In 1961, Alan Shepard was the first American to fly into outer space. In 1962, John Glenn was the first American to orbit the earth. In 1969, Apollo 11 carried Americans to the moon. Neil Armstrong was the first person to set foot on the moon, followed by Edwin "Buzz" Aldrin.[9] Space flight had become a reality.
- On May 30, 2020, for the first time in nine years, NASA astronauts were launched from American soil on a mission to the International Space Station. For the first time in history, those astronauts flew on a privately owned and operated reusable rocket.[10] The race to the stars has begun in earnest.
- Artificial intelligence is increasing by leaps and bounds. Each year car manufacturers offer additional smart-auto technology features to assist drivers. No fully autonomous (self-driving or driverless) vehicles operate legally on our roads today, but it seems this reality is just a matter of time.
- Christian ministry has also advanced due to advances in technology. The advent of radio and television signals transmitted by satellites and self-contained, solar-powered audio and video equipment has enabled ministries to flourish around the world, particularly in regions where electronic technology has been sparse or absent. Don and Julie, friends of mine engaged in missionary ministry, told me about a solar-powered audio/video system that connects to smartphones and is being used to present the gospel to tribes in Africa in their native language. What an awesome tool to be used for the kingdom of heaven.

However, technological advances have a down side as well. I have received emails from individuals containing statements I know they would not have said if we were talking in person. Since email allows the two communicating parties to be separated, typed words can be more thoughtless, haphazard, or callous compared to words spoken at close quarters. Furthermore, emails convey a more restricted message to recipients as opposed to a direct conversation. With email you do not get, for example, the sender's body language or voice inflection. With advances in technology, it seems to me the art of face-to-face communication is decreasing.

I was in a restaurant with a friend one evening. Four young women were sitting at a table a short distance away. All four of them were texting, occasionally laughing or making short comments, but for the most part, it was constant texting. I wondered why people who know each other would choose to get together and then ignore each other. After a few minutes I realized they weren't ignoring each other. They were texting each other, which confused me even more. I simply cannot understand why anyone would sit face to face with others and communicate with them by typing rather than speaking. One thing I do understand is this type of communication seems to be here to stay. However, I am convinced one-on-one, face-to-face communication, to the extent it is practical, is the most intimate and effective way of presenting the gospel message.

Just as electronic technology has drawbacks, so does human communication. As we all know, the human tongue is truly a double-edged sword. Scripture tells us:

- "With the tongue we praise our Lord and Father, and with it we curse human beings, who have been made in God's likeness." (James 3:9)
- "The tongue also is a fire, a world of evil among the parts of the body. It corrupts the whole body, sets the whole course of one's life on fire, and is itself set on fire by hell." (James 3:6)

Free speech is foundational to who we are as Americans. I am thankful we have the First Amendment to the Constitution. However, as Christians, God does not give us "free reign" to say whatever we think because not all our thoughts are godly. Even when we have pure intentions, our words can be unwise or untimely. Once reckless words are spoken, they cannot be taken back. The damage is permanent. When it comes to communication, we must be deliberate, restraining our tongues as we engage the world. Before we speak, we need to consider very deliberately not only what we are about to say but how, why, and when we say it.

Scripture sets the bar high regarding the words we speak. "Let your conversation be always full of grace, seasoned with salt, so that you may know how to answer everyone" (Colossians 4:6). Speaking the truth in love is a simple concept, but it is difficult for flawed humans to employ. Most of us are pretty good at speaking the truth. It is the "in love" part that seems elusive, particularly if we are angry, disagree with someone, or the topic at hand is distasteful to us.

Some carry a seemingly hate-filled message in the name of Christianity, desiring God's fiery judgment. A US Courts article, "Facts and Case Summary—Snyder v. Phelps," says,

> Fred Phelps and his followers at the Westboro Baptist Church believe that God punishes the United States for its tolerance of homosexuality, particularly within the military. To demonstrate their beliefs, Phelps and his followers often picket at military funerals. Albert Snyder's son, Lance Corporal Matthew Snyder, was killed in the line of duty in Iraq in 2006. Westboro picketed Matthew Snyder's funeral displaying signs that stated, for instance, "God Hates the USA/Thank God for 9/11," "Thank God for Dead Soldiers," and "Don't Pray for the USA." . . . Snyder sued Phelps and the church claiming, among other things, that their actions caused him severe emotional distress.[11]

Believers should not relish the impending eternal torment of those who reject Jesus Christ as Lord. Remember, God does hate sin, but he loves the sinner, including you.

After Hurricane Katrina devastated portions of New Orleans in 2005, I heard more than one Christian comment how this natural disaster was God's judgment on the city because of the sins of people there. I don't know if God caused or allowed Hurricane Katrina to happen, but he did one or the other. Again, I don't understand how believers determined God caused this disaster because of the sinful actions of those people. From a purely human perspective, at least one thing bothers me about this proposed theory. If God wanted to use a hurricane to punish the "worst of the worst" in New Orleans, why was the French Quarter, renowned as the most decadent part of the city, spared from most of the storm damage?

Those Christians whose message dwells on God's wrath speak the truth, but only in part. God is sovereign over all. God will judge and punish sin, either here on earth, on Judgment Day or both. Since God is sovereign, I believe he either allows or causes everything that happens on earth. Some reasons people suffer on earth are as follows.

- We live in a fallen, decaying world, just like our bodies, because it is filled with sin. This condition produces calamities, such as hurricanes, floods, disease, famine, crime, and death. God allows these things as a result of the sin humankind willfully chose to bring into the world when Eve and Adam disobeyed.
- Poor choices can bring us misery. For example, some have chosen to drive while drunk. A drunk driver crashes into an oncoming car, killing others and getting sentenced to prison. God allows these things because of our sinful choices.
- Satan tempts people to encourage them to sin (1 Corinthians 7:5). God allows this to happen because humankind willfully chose to bring sin into the world.
- Satan persecutes people for his own evil purposes (Job 2:3–6). God allows these things to happen for his glory.
- Sometimes God decides to punish people on earth because of their sins. I will use biblical examples since I have no firsthand knowledge of punishments God has pronounced on earth during my lifetime. God destroyed Sodom and Gomorrah because of their sin (Genesis 19:24–25). He struck Ananias and Sapphira dead because they lied to his Spirit (Acts 5:3–5, 7–10). God caused these things to happen.
- The difference between Satan's temptations and God's tests is the intent. God's intent is for the people being tested to pass the test, bringing glory to God. Satan's intent is for the people being tempted to fail. Whenever a believer is tempted by Satan, God has provided a way out, so the Christian can escape without sinning (1 Corinthians 10:13).

I am convinced most "bad things" that happen to people on earth are not caused by God. They are caused by living in a sinful world and by our sinful nature. So, what is the message I should be communicating to a lost world? I must be consistently diligent, as much as humanly possible, to take captive every thought entering my mind, scrutinizing each of them in the light of God's Word and Spirit. Then, if I decide to comment on a particular thought, I will be able to speak the truth in love, with humility for the benefit of all. As believers we know our God is loving as well as wrathful. We also understand a day of judgment is coming. Therefore, the message of the kingdom of God is such good news. As ambassadors from the kingdom of heaven speaking to the lost, our primary message needs to be about God's unfailing love and forgiveness.

Showing the Truth in Love

What we say and how we say it are very important. Equally important is how we show the truth in love. The Internet and bookstores are replete with articles and books detailing the problems with Christianity in America, resulting in its irrelevancy. Christians in America can always improve regarding their interaction with the world. After all, 100 percent of the Body of Christ is composed of flawed humans. However, Christianity has not been and is not irrelevant anywhere on this planet.

For just a moment, let's look only at the monetary impact of the Body of Christ on the needy in America. In an article called "Religion Contributes $1.2 Trillion to US Economy, More Than Top 10 Tech Companies Combined, Study Finds," Brandon Showalter says a Georgetown University released a study in 2016 indicating religious groups, including religious institutions, faith-based charities, and businesses inspired by faith, contribute $1.2 trillion to the US economy. Michael Grim, co-author of the study, said this is the first documented quantitative analysis of the economic impact of religion. Grim further notes "in an age where there's a growing belief that religion is not a positive for American society, adding up the numbers is a tangible reminder of the impact of religion"[12]

Economic impact is only one part of the equation. In addition to the monetary contribution by religious groups to the needy in America, consider the value of Christian organizations helping pregnant women choose adoption rather than abortion, believers who serve as foster parents or adopt orphaned children, and needy persons who decide to accept Jesus Christ as Lord and Savior because of the kindness they were shown while they were in need. Across America, tens of thousands of Christian organizations and individuals are ministering to "the least of these" at home and abroad. Christians exhibiting love is not irrelevant in America. It is vital and life-changing for those who serve and for those who are being served.

CHAPTER 13

Retirement—A Golden Opportunity

> Even when I am old and gray, do not forsake me, my God, till I declare your power to the next generation, your mighty acts to all who are to come. (Psalm 71:18)

I don't recall when I first gave serious thought to retirement. Certainly, by the time I was established in my work career, my financial plan for retirement had begun as I started contributing to a retirement savings account. I imagine most Americans who are financially able have made or are making plans for their retirement as well. We all expect, or at least hope, we will be prepared financially for this season of our lives. It is good to look forward to a time when we will not be required to labor in order to provide for our basic needs. Practically speaking, retirement is a matter of financial resources, not age. A sixty-five-year-old person who doesn't have the money to pay the bills will have to continue to work. Conversely, a person who is a multi-millionaire by age thirty could retire if he or she chose to do so. Some people work their entire adult lives and die without ever having the opportunity to retire from the workforce. Others never retire because they love their work.

Many of us spend most of our lives in a predictable pattern of preparing for the next stage in life. From birth until age twenty-two or so, we are growing into adulthood and being educated to prepare us for a career. We spend the next forty or more years working to build a career, family, and home and prepare for retirement. Then, suddenly, the kids have left home, and we retire from the workplace, if we are fortunate enough. So, what's next for those who do retire one day? What's the next stage once I have ceased employment permanently? Some say, "Nothing." They view retirement as a time of complete leisure, pursuing various hobbies. Hopefully, believers are continuing to prepare for eternity, as they have been their entire Christian lives. I wonder how often we, as followers of Christ, ask ourselves, "What would God have me do when I no longer have to work forty hours or more per week to earn a paycheck?"

I have also considered how tithing relates to retirement, if at all. Presumably, those who tithe (give the first 10 percent of their earnings to the Lord) understand this practice is a scriptural command and that we bring glory to God when we cheerfully comply. Is the concept of tithing limited to earnings only? How much time should those who are employed full time devote to the Lord's work? I've discussed this topic with a few close friends who love the Lord and know Scripture much better than I do. It seems to me, if the Lord wants me to give at least 10 percent of my earnings to benefit his kingdom, wouldn't the Lord also want me to give at least 10 percent of the equivalent time I spent laboring for money to his work as well? (I'm not including attending worship services, Sunday school, and prayer meetings here.) Following this logic, if I do give 10 percent of my time to the Lord's work while employed full time and am blessed with the opportunity to retire, how much time should I give to the Lord's work then? Should it be more, less, or the same as when I was employed?

Don't misunderstand me on this point. I am not insinuating that believers should give forty or fifty hours a week to the Lord's work (though may God bless you mightily if you decide to do so). I am not trying to tell anyone what or how much they should do. What I am suggesting is, each of us should consider this matter. Should we continue, after retirement, to devote at least part of our time, talent, and treasures to the Lord's work? Some Christians are the sole full-time caregivers to debilitated or handicapped relatives or friends. If so, God bless you for your service to the kingdom of heaven in that capacity. While ministering at home, you could also choose to be a prayer warrior for your local body of Christ. You may want to take up golf. Go have fun on the links, but while you are there, look for opportunities the Holy Spirit might provide you to witness to someone. Form a foursome with three lost souls, and become their friend. You may want to be part of a bridge club. Great, go and witness there as you play. Surely your local church body could use your skills one or five, days a week in some capacity. If you prefer, engage in these leisure activities with no agenda, just for the fun of it. Then carve out some time during your week to engage in a specific activity that fits your God-given gifts to promote the kingdom of heaven.

I have two questions, one general and one specific, for more mature believers. First, why do you think God gave us the most time, experience, and wisdom all at once? Second, why did God place us in this time during a dark period of upheaval and turmoil in our homeland in our last days of life on earth? I am convinced God has shaped us for a specific ministry, positioned us exactly when and where he wants us to be, and endowed us with gifts and skills that can only be attained through trial by fire and the passage of time for his good purpose. Think about it; God has given us the precious gifts of:

- Suffering through decades of pain, disease, death, and sorrow;
- A deep well of wisdom from studying and applying the Bible;
- Living victoriously through decades of applying God's Word to battle our sinful nature and defeat Satan's lies;
- Humility produced by the losses in battle and the resulting knowledge that we can only succeed in Jesus Christ;
- His Spirit shaping our character and talents, for decades, so we look more like Jesus than we ever have before; and
- Decades of experience building one-on-one relationships.

It is encouraging to know others who love the Lord have spent time deliberating on this issue. In his book, *Finding Favor*, Brian Jones interprets a statement by Christian philosopher Elton Trueblood saying,

> God wants us to view every area of our lives as holy ground. Your boardroom, . . . baby's nursery, . . . venture capital meeting is holy ground. It's all holy ground in the eyes of the Lord. But part of doing holy work includes doing it the way it was meant to be done: with every ounce of our beings as an act of worship . . . Half-hearted efforts at raising a teenager won't cut it. Neither will approaching retirement without a plan for how you'll use your most unrestricted years to serve God.[1]

Suffering

Usually, those who have lived longer tend to have endured more suffering. But young or old, I don't know many who think about suffering as a "gift." What human in their right mind would choose suffering as a ministry? Jesus. (Yes, I know he was fully God, but he was also fully human). His primary objective while on earth was to seek and save the lost. To achieve his Father's objective, Jesus knew he would have to suffer and die. He also knew he was the only one who could achieve God's plan of salvation for humankind. We don't talk much about the heinous brutality of Jesus's death, but in a single verse, the prophet Isaiah gives us a brief but graphic glimpse of Jesus's torture: "Just as there were many who were appalled at him—his appearance was so disfigured beyond that of any human being and his form marred beyond human likeness" (Isaiah 52:14).

Let those last four words of Isaiah's description sink in. I don't want to dwell on suffering as a gift, nor do I want to dwell on Jesus's suffering. In 2004, our local body of Christ and another reserved two movie theaters, so we could go as a group by ourselves to watch *The Passion of the Christ*. The local television station heard about our private showing and was waiting outside as we left the theater. One of the moviegoers was asked, "Why did you want to watch the movie alone rather than attend a public showing?"

"For the same reason you sit on the 'home side' of the field when you attend a football game at home," the person responded. "You want to be surrounded by those who are rooting for the same team as you."

Another question posed was "How would you describe the movie?"

The response was, "It was the most gut-wrenching love story ever told."

This movie focused on the last twelve hours of Jesus's life leading to his death, portraying the savage torture, mockery, and crucifixion in graphic detail. I knew I was watching a movie, and Jim Caviezel, who portrayed Jesus, was not being hurt. Nonetheless, I don't think there was a dry eye in the theater. The moving part was the object of the beating rather than the brutal beating itself. But the most moving part was the reminder of my shame, knowing it was my sin (which I had yet to commit at the time of the crucifixion) that caused the brutal torture of my Lord some two thousand years ago. I would love to be able to say the first-century Roman rulers and Jewish leaders were responsible for Jesus's crucifixion, but I can't because it isn't true. Jesus didn't just die for the sins of first-century humans. He died for my sins too. My sins nailed Jesus to the cross as much as the Roman soldier with the hammer and spikes did. Yours did too.

In his book, *Radical,* David Platt exquisitely conveys the message of Jesus's suffering through the crucifixion.

> What happened at the Cross was not primarily about nails being thrust into Jesus's hands and feet but about the wrath due your sin and my sin being thrust upon his soul. In that holy moment, all the righteous wrath and justice of God due us came rushing down like a torrent on Christ himself. Some say, 'God looked down and could not bear to see the suffering that the soldiers were inflicting upon Jesus, so he turned away.' But this is not true. God turned away because he could not bear to see your sin and my sin on his Son.[2]

Jesus's excruciating suffering produced the greatest possible good for humankind while also bringing glory to God. Likewise, God can use our suffering to bring glory to him and further his kingdom. When Christians suffer for their faith or suffer through no fault of their own and persevere, they bring glory to God. Our suffering can also be used in ministry to the saved and the lost. As Paul told the believers in Corinth, "As God comforts us in all our troubles, we can comfort those in any trouble with the comfort we ourselves receive from God (1 Corinthians 1:3–5).

On numerous occasions my buddy Rick has said, "Three of the most powerful words in ministry are, 'What, you too?'" Rick was burned badly as a boy over a significant portion of his body. To this day he bears the scars from his accident. When Rick goes to visit burn patients in the hospital, he has instant credibility with those patients because of his scars. Even before Rick speaks, patients know he has already gone through the same suffering they are experiencing. Their pain doesn't come only from the salt-water debridement, skin grafts, and the extended healing process. It also comes from how they are being treated and will be treated by some people in the future because they will look different for the rest of their lives. When Rick encourages them, they know his words are true, coming from someone intimately familiar with their ordeal. These burn patients look at Rick and say, "What, you too?" They understand he has not only survived but flourished. Then they are encouraged because they realize they can do the same.

The story of Charles "Chuck" Colson, former White House counsel to President Richard M. Nixon, is a testimony to God's grace and mercy. As a new Christian, Colson voluntarily pled guilty to obstruction of justice in 1974 and served seven months in Alabama's Maxwell Prison for his part in the Watergate scandal. Colson emerged from prison with a new mission: mobilizing the Christian church to minister to prisoners. He founded Prison Fellowship in 1976, now the nation's largest Christian nonprofit serving prisoners, former prisoners, and their families and a leading advocate for criminal justice reform. Chuck Colson passed away April 21, 2012. His legacy continues, however, in the work of Prison Fellowship and in the lives of the many people his ministry has touched.[4]

What a topsy-turvy life Colson led. In the prime of his life, he rubbed shoulders with some of the most powerful people in America. But one day he found himself being sentenced to prison. Then, while in prison, God called him to serve his fellow inmates. Colson went from a sinful power broker to an inmate to a godly legacy still impacting America years after his death, from earthly suffering to a ministry for the kingdom of God. All of us have dealt, or will deal with, pain, suffering, and discouragement of many kinds. We each need to ask ourselves; how can I use this painful season in my life to help someone else? How can I use this to bring glory to God? We need to search diligently for ways to make our temporary suffering an eternal gain for others, just like Jesus did.

A Legacy of Godliness

In his book, *The Tender Warrior*, Stu Weber says,

In our culture, when we think of provision, we think of food on the table and a roof over our heads . . . We revert to the things we can see, when in fact it is the unseen world, the world of the spirit, the world of relationships, where we ought to be majoring in our provision. Matters of character, heart, spirit, integrity, justice, humility—the kinds of things that last. The character traits that outlive a man and leave, not a monument, but a legacy.[3]

Legacy, heritage, and inheritance are closely related terms, used interchangeably at times. One distinction I make between legacy and heritage is the giver or donor is the one who has developed the legacy being given. To the recipient, the legacy being received is known as a heritage. I have always considered an inheritance to be tangible, while heritage and a legacy are something intangible, such as traditions. Each of us, Christian and non-Christian alike, will leave a legacy of one kind or another. A godly legacy is not confined to the great theologians or outstanding evangelists. It does not require advanced education or a ministerial degree. The best legacy a Christian can leave is the example of a life where godly wisdom is applied to daily living. When my parents died, I inherited tangible things, i.e., stuff. Long before they died, they established a legacy of godliness through love and devotion to their Lord Jesus Christ and their fellow people. Their invaluable legacy became my heritage.

With each passing generation in America, more and more children are growing up in homes where either one or both parents (if they have two parents in their home) do not know Jesus Christ as Lord and Savior. In such cases, the legacy left by the non-Christian parent is very different from the Christian parent. I am not inferring non-Christian parents are leaving a bad legacy, but a worldly legacy, no matter how "good" it is, will not be Christ-centered. The eternal ramifications between these two types of legacies are enormous.

Consider the following contrasts between the worldview (this is a generalization and certainly does not apply to all non-Christians) in America today compared to a "Christ view" (or biblical worldview).

- The world says, "He who dies with the most toys wins." God says, "You can't serve both God and money" (Matthew 6:24).
- The world says, "Winning isn't everything; it's the only thing." God says, "So the last will be first, and the first will be last" (Matthew 20:16).
- The world says, "Do unto others before they do unto you." God says, "Do to others as you would have them do to you" (Luke 6:31).
- The world says, "A friend in need is a pest indeed." God says, "The greatest among you will be your servant (Matthew 23:11).

These two views are not simply different; they are complete opposites. Many of those who are lost will reject the lifestyle and attitudes of believers. Some of those who are lost will view the Christian lifestyle as a rejection and even a condemnation of their way of life. Such people do not want to hear about a "right" way to live and a "wrong" way to live. Those who want to engage in a non-heterosexual lifestyle are intent on being able to "marry."

They don't want a civil union. They want to be "married," so their lifestyle will be considered normal, accepted by everyone as right.

It was God Almighty who ordained marriage as one man and one woman for their lifetime. I understand those Christians who say same-gender unions should not be called "marriage" because of God's definition. I also understand if the United States government or courts decide to redefine marriage, they have the worldly right to do so. This is not a condemnation of those who choose one lifestyle over another. According to God's Word, those who engage in same-sex lifestyles are sinners. I am a sinner too. My sins are simply different from their sins. We will all give an account one day.

We see the "bandwagon approach" being applied regularly today to convince everyone to accept other people's lifestyle choices. The message is, everyone else is either doing it or accepting it. Therefore, you should too. If the bandwagon approach is unsuccessful, the assumption is those who object are bigoted, discriminatory, intolerant, and outdated. Therefore, such detractors must be "persuaded" to rethink their antiquated position and comply with the new norms.

How is the godliness of Christians exhibited to others in a distinct way? What makes believers "peculiar" to the rest of the world? One of the more prominent differences between Christians and the lost is that saved souls possess joy and peace even in a world of chaos and uncertainty. Hopefully, our families will recognize our godliness over time and choose to incorporate godliness by accepting Jesus Christ as Lord and Savior. However, this legacy is not for them alone. Many others who are not family members will also witness our lives. We should want them to be pointed to Christ by our example and choose to give their lives to Christ.

Most of us probably know one or more believers who epitomize the joy and peace we have in Jesus Christ. Lona was a vivacious woman who loved the Lord. She came to services prepared to worship and always exuded joy and peace. Lona was "just happy to be there," and her attitude was infectious. Some of us know one or more Christians whose countenance, words, and actions do not display joy or peace. They appear unhappy to be where they are. Most Christians fall somewhere in between. Mom had two standard phrases to describe the grumpy or perpetually angry group. She would say, "That man looked like he could chew nails and spit fire," or "That woman's face would curdle milk." Mom never explained the distinction, if any, between these two. It didn't matter. I got the point. We know life is hard. As we get older, and health issues begin to add up, life gets even more difficult. Nonetheless, Christians are supposed to possess, and hopefully convey, joy and peace. We shouldn't be resentful and argumentative. So, to the grumpy group, are you saved by grace? Are you indwelt by the Spirit of God? Do you get to spend eternity with Jesus one day? If the answer is "yes," then let those facts light up your countenance. We need the lost world to see our peace and joy.

True peace and joy are rare commodities in our world, and they're becoming rarer each day. Lost souls may define peace as the absence of war or strife. They tend to describe happiness in an attempt to define joy. What the lost refer to as peace and joy are the result of external factors, worldly conditions. Some worldly events do contribute to happiness, such as the birth of a healthy child or the wedding of a grown child who has found true love. Other worldly factors can contribute to temporary peace, such as when the family is healthy, everyone is successfully pursuing their dreams, work is going great, and no one in the family is fighting. When things are going well, "all is at peace with the world," as some might say. But what the world calls peace and joy are guaranteed to be temporary at best. Those who place their trust in things—a great job, a luxurious car, a large stock portfolio—will always worry about those temporary things. The job may be lost due to downsizing. The car will rust, or the engine will give out eventually. The stock market is unstable, rising and falling like a yo-yo. Trying desperately to hold onto the temporary is a losing battle filled with anxiety and unrest.

Believers need to focus not on the temporary but on things imperishable and true, the love, faithfulness, and promises of God. For Christians, neither peace nor joy come from external factors or worldly conditions. Our joy and peace come from within, from the indwelling Spirit of God. Our joy comes from believing in God and being in his presence. Our eternity with him is secure no matter what happens on earth. God's Word reminds us that worldly trials and tribulations should not impact our joy. James tells us we are to remain joyful in the face of "trials of many kinds" (James 1:2). Jesus is our peace because, on the cross, he reconciled us to God. Jesus told us, "Peace I leave with you; my peace I give you. I do not give to you as the world gives. Do not let your hearts be troubled and do not be afraid" (John 14:27). Jesus's peace had to be different from the world's peace since Jesus was the only one who could pay the price for our sins.

Since our peace and joy come from God, they should not be impacted by external factors. Because God's Spirit resides within believers, we should exude the fruit of the Spirit, including joy and peace, daily. We cannot adequately explain our joy to the world since the message of the cross is foolishness to those who are perishing, nor can we explain God's peace, which transcends all understanding (Philippians 4:7). It would be like trying to explain what chocolate tastes like to someone who has never tasted it, explaining it so perfectly that the person could taste the chocolate in their mouth. They must taste it themselves to understand it. We are called to point the way for those who desire to taste. Saint Thomas Aquinas has been credited with saying, "To one who has faith, no explanation is necessary. To one without faith, no explanation is possible." Our families, friends, and neighbors need to witness our legacy of godly living, to see something uniquely different from the increasingly godless culture in America. If given the opportunity, we should be willing to explain the reason for our lifestyle. Even if no one ever asks for an explanation, those lost souls who witness our lives should perceive something different about us, something desirable and maybe even peculiar.

CHAPTER 14

Your Assigned Area of Operation

Then Jesus came to them and said, "All authority in heaven and on earth has been given to me. Therefore, go and make disciples of all nations, baptizing them in the name of the Father and of the Son and of the Holy Spirit, and teaching them to obey everything I have commanded you. And surely, I am with you always, to the very end of the age." (Matthew 28:18–20)

Ministering in Far-Away Places

Most of us have read books and articles or heard stories about missionaries, at least some of the more famous ones. I am familiar with a few of these, including Mother Teresa who served the poorest in India; Hudson Taylor, a missionary to China; and Jim Elliot, an American missionary to Ecuador who was martyred there. On a more personal note, I have had the opportunity to become acquainted with two American missionary families who served in foreign countries.

Jim and Becky were serving as missionaries in Grenada. During May 1996 eight people, me included, traveled to Grenada to help with the construction of a church building. The island was lovely and the surrounding sea was inviting, but the paradise ended there. Plentiful drinking water, electricity, indoor plumbing, good schools, and adequate medical facilities, all things I had taken for granted in America, were luxuries there. At the time of my visit, Grenada was a matriarchal society. Sexual purity and marriage were uncommon practices. Jim and Becky were trying to model a Christian family life for the people there. Crime was also a significant problem. Sometimes Jim and Becky had grave concerns for their safety. One evening as I sat talking with Jim, he said the greatest sacrifice he and Becky made for missionary work was to leave their extended families.

This mission trip provided me with several eye-opening realizations. Two of these were the abject poverty suffered by many Grenadians and the sacrifice of time with loved ones made by the missionaries. I have seen poverty in America. The Appalachian Mountains, covering a significant portion of West Virginia, are inhabited by some of the poorest people in the United States. I lived in Hugheston, West Virginia, a small coal-mining community, for four years. Once a month the government would deliver "commodities" to a small building in Hugheston. Those people whose low income qualified them would come to the building to receive a ration of flour, cheese, beans, and other food staples. There was no distribution of commodities by the government in Grenada. Jim said if not for the fruit trees, which produced fruit almost year-round, the poorest in Grenada might starve.

That one-week mission trip changed me, and I am grateful for it. I went on the trip thinking I would give something to the people of Grenada and the missionaries. I did contribute what I could through a week of labor, but I received so much more in return. I see and think differently now in a way that could only be accomplished by my exposure to those people and their land. Our Lord has a funny way of doing things, like blessing me when I thought I was going to be a blessing to others. Two other things I learned on that trip were how rich I am in material things and how little I truly sacrifice for the Lord's work.

I got to know another missionary family quite well. Dan and Meg serve as missionaries in a foreign land thousands of miles from their home, family, and friends. They minister to a group of non-Christian people whose leadership is adamantly opposed to any type of outside influence. When sighted in public, the locals know instantly that Dan and Meg are not one of their own. They must work tirelessly, seeking any opportunity to present the message of the kingdom of heaven. Imagine the frustration generated by their sacrifice and the isolation they experience daily. I have told Dan and Meg on more than one occasion that I'm glad they do what they do because I don't think I could. To me, they are heroes in the faith, ordinary folk who love Jesus and allow the Holy Spirit to do extraordinary things through them for God's glory.

One significant difficulty for anyone engaged in missionary work in a land with few Christians is fellowship with other believers. The gathering of like-minded Christ followers, with whom we can worship, study, and encourage each other is of vital importance. I wonder if we don't take the local body of Christ for granted sometimes. I'm certain missionaries like Jim, Becky, Dan, and Meg do not. Some Christians are called by the Lord to serve in places far from where they were born or raised. For years my idea of a missionary was one who served the Lord in a country other than where they were born or raised. God's view of a missionary has never been so limited. Every place you set your foot on this earth is your mission field. We are called to minister wherever we are and wherever we go each day.

Ministering at Home

The primary lifelong ministry of all believers is to establish an intimate relationship with God through Jesus Christ. For those who are married, the second-most important ministry is to our spouses (Ephesians 5:25–28). When I married Susie, I took vows before God when I said "I do." I promised God I would "love, honor, and cherish" Susie. I was called as a husband and a father to live a godly life and give glory to God by pointing my family toward Jesus Christ. For those who are mothers or fathers, the third-most important ministry is to our children. Susie and I, as father and mother, were called to teach God's commandments to our children (Deuteronomy 11:18–21). Most Christians are called to multiple ministries during their lifetime. Some occur at the same time. I am convinced that when God calls me to multiple ministries, he will never call me to significantly reduce or abandon my ministry within my own home.

Ministering Where You Are as You Go

Mary and Joseph took Jesus to Egypt as a young child and later returned to live in Nazareth in Galilee. Otherwise, Jesus stayed within walking distance of his earthly birthplace, literally. Jesus was not a world traveler by anyone's measure. However, the distance Jesus traveled was not important. What mattered was, he ministered where he was as he went. Likewise, how far or how little we travel is of no importance. What we do as we travel is what counts. Every place we go—the workplace, the supermarket, the gym, driving on the highway, and on business trips out of town—is our "nation," our assigned area of operation as ambassadors. As kingdom of heaven ambassadors at large on Earth, our mission field is wherever we are today.

When you minister where you are, as you go, a great variety of opportunities are available to you. The service area you decide to engage in is between you and the Lord. I have always desired to engage in at least two different ministries, if possible, one within the Body of Christ and one outside the Body of Christ. I have always searched for ministries with significant needs for volunteers and where the field is "ripe for harvest." In this manner, I can engage in evangelizing the lost and building up the Body of Christ. In my opinion, a biblical mission statement for any local congregation should contain these two objectives at a minimum. Regardless of our personal experiences, natural affinities, or spiritual gifts, we all can participate in different ways to help build up the Body of Christ. We can all pray for, encourage, and serve the local congregation, to name just a few.

I would also like to mention one ministry area I consider to be of vital importance to the Body of Christ as a whole. Furthermore, every believer can participate in this ministry. Each member of the local body of Christ needs to fully support their leadership. Should we complain to the leadership when things are going wrong within the congregation? Yes, and rightly so since they are responsible for shepherding the flock. Conversely, we should be just as willing to compliment the leadership for their efforts to do things right. Do we expect the leadership to be dedicated to evangelizing the lost and building up the Body of Christ? Certainly. We should be eagerly engaging in positive words and deeds, affirming their efforts in this regard. Answer these two questions for yourself. When was the last time you sincerely complimented someone in leadership, not because the person did something for you but simply because the person was diligently serving, attempting to do what was right? When was the last time you asked someone in leadership "How can I help to achieve the goals set by the leadership?" with the firm intent of actually helping them reach those goals?

Why would I choose to discuss this? I'm glad you asked. One reason is leaders don't usually bring up this subject. They earnestly desire to be affirmed, like every human, but will not ask for it because it may make them seem self-centered or glory seeking. The real reason for me is because we are engaged in spiritual warfare, and our enemy has targeted our leaders. I am convinced beyond a shadow of doubt that:

- Spiritual warfare in America (and around the world) is increasing exponentially today. Numerous passages in Scripture describe the increasing evil and carnage of spiritual warfare waged by Satan against God and those who believe in his Son, Jesus, in the last days.
- The devil, a master strategist of warfare, knows wounding or killing the leaders in a local body of Christ will likely result in significant "collateral damage." We see the truth of this even from a human perspective. If I can maim or kill either a private or a general in the opposing army, but not both, I will usually, if not always, choose the general.
- Collateral damage may include diminished faith or possibly even rejected faith in Jesus Christ because of the damage done to the leadership.
- The leadership of a local body of Christ live in a "glass house." Everything they say and do, as well as their immediate family, is subjected to additional scrutiny, as if they should be less sinful or held to a higher standard. If they should be held to a higher standard (James 3:1), it is God's place to do so, not ours.

How do we show support for our leaders? Some simple ways include praying for them, encouraging them with spoken words and notes, celebrating with them in their successes, and empathizing with them in their struggles and failures. The staff are usually hard workers. They're certainly not in ministry to get rich. The leaders who are not on staff, such as elders, deacons, and lay ministers, to name only a few, serve for no pay and still must deal with all the struggles of the congregation. A dear friend of mine who was serving as an elder at the time was speaking at a Christian men's breakfast. He said, "The best part of serving in leadership is the people. The worst part of serving in leadership is the people."

We can either be a tremendous asset or a liability to the leadership of a congregation. The choice is ours. When someone in leadership sees me walking toward them, I don't want them to look for someplace to hide or wish they could. My desire is they would be glad to see me and spend a little time with me. This is not an attempt to deny reality. On occasion, tough subjects need to be discussed with one or more of the leaders. However, such a conversation should be conducted with the same love and respect you would show to your grandparents if you were talking to them. To my regret, not all my conversations as a young Christian were loving and gentle.

If I do not have full faith in the leadership of the local body of Christ, I need to find a body where I can have full faith. Scripture says, "Have confidence in your leaders and submit to their authority, because they keep watch over you as those who must give an account. Do this so their work will be a joy, not a burden, for that would be of no benefit to you" (Hebrews 13:17). We are to make the leaders' job a joy! I am supposed to desire to follow my leaders. If I am on the battlefield, I don't want my officers injured or killed, even if I am left unharmed. Their injury or death only places me at greater risk because the enemy is lurking nearby, waiting for another opportunity to attack. Remember, when one part of the body suffers, we all suffer.

A Unique Opportunity in America

This world has been groaning and continues to groan as it decays from sin. Furthermore, believers groan inwardly as we eagerly await the redemption of our bodies in eternity. Meanwhile, the persecution of Christians has existed since Jesus's public ministry began. Since the first century, the death of Christianity has been plotted, predicted, and proclaimed. While every generation of humans has seen this persecution of Christianity, none have seen the death of it, nor will any generation ever see such an occurrence.

Christians in America have been insulated to a great degree from the extreme persecution Christians face in other countries around the world. However, American believers who have studied the Bible know, or should have known, the storm of Christian persecution would come to our shores sooner or later. It's here now, and the odds of it going away are slim and none. For the first time in my life, I see unprecedented and systemic chaos, hatred, violence, and division in my homeland. To be sure, the violence I saw in America during the 1960s was intense. The issue at the time was equality for blacks in our nation. The violence and chaos we see today differs significantly. It appears to be random, seemingly fomented by a generalized lawlessness against any established rule or tradition.

As we have already discussed, people around the world are being attacked, imprisoned, and killed simply because they are Christians. With increasing hostility toward Christians growing in America, it begs the question, to what extent are believers in our country willing to suffer for their faith if and when required? I ask myself, "What have I had to sacrifice for my faith?" The honest response is, "Very little." I've never been beaten or imprisoned. I've never lost a job or had property confiscated because of my beliefs. Then I ask myself, "Would I continue in my faith if it cost me much, or everything?" Again, the honest response is "I hope so." But I'm not 100 percent sure. I've never had to endure a test anything like these persecuted believers.

As I have talked with brothers and sisters in Christ, some have suggested the US government should be more active in protecting Christian rights, particularly since we were founded as a Christian nation. While such a notion may be sincere, I believe it is based on an erroneous assumption and is unrealistic considering the past actions of our government. Regarding the erroneous assumption, the First Amendment to the US Constitution says, "Congress shall make no law respecting an establishment of religion, or prohibiting the free exercise thereof; or abridging the freedom of speech."[1] If I read the First Amendment correctly, the US government cannot give preferential treatment to one religion over another. It is to protect the free exercise of religion for all religions equally. The US government has, in fact, increasingly taken actions that can be interpreted as an attempt to remove Christian speech and theology from the public square. We have every reason to conclude our government has no intention of protecting Christian beliefs, nor can we expect God to protect us from persecution since his Word says we will be persecuted for our faith.

While Jesus walked the earth, the Jewish people were enslaved, subject to the Roman Empire, which oppressed the Jewish people and Christians. Scripture does not record any instance when Jesus suggested believers should petition the Roman government for protection from religious persecution, nor did Jesus involve himself in the political affairs of his day. He simply went about his Father's business every day, regardless of the government's actions toward him, until his job was completed.

After Jesus's ascension, the earliest believers made their choice, through the Holy Spirit's guidance, regarding how best to witness in a sinful, hostile world. It's our turn to decide what to do. How will we present the good news of the gospel while simultaneously navigating this storm of animosity and, in some cases, hate? Hopefully, our response to these questions will be, "Just like Jesus did." He and his followers faced far more hostility and hatred than most American believers have, and Jesus told us what to expect because of our faith in him. Jesus told his followers that they would be hated and persecuted, even unto death, because of him. Those two truths, faith in Jesus and persecution because of Christian faith, are inseparable.

Jesus said the following to his disciples.

- "You will be hated by everyone because of me." (Matthew 10:22)
- "You will be handed over to be persecuted and put to death, and you will be hated by all nations because of me." (Matthew 24:9)
- "Blessed are you when people insult you, persecute you and falsely say all kinds of evil against you because of me." (Matthew 5:11)
- "If the world hates you, keep in mind that it hated me first . . . Remember what I told you . . . If they persecuted me, they will persecute you also." (John 15:18–20)
- "Blessed are you when people hate you, when they exclude you and insult you and reject your name as evil, because of the Son of Man" (Luke 6:22).

So, for what purpose do we rejoice in these fiery ordeals? Peter's response is, "In all this you greatly rejoice so . . . our faith will be proven genuine (I Peter 1:6–7). Intense spiritual warfare is taking place all around us, and it is increasing as we speak. Scripture clearly explains how cruel and ungodly the last days will be and how the pattern will increase until the Lord returns. We have all seen the increasing ungodliness in America for decades. We need to as, the Lord how he would use us in this war, at this time, where we are. Whatever comes our way, we should not fear. First, God is in control. We who believe in Jesus Christ are on the winning side. Nothing can change that. Second, God has transformed us by placing within us his spirit of power, not timidity. David, a deeply flawed human who loved the Lord, explains the result of this transformation by posing two questions and then providing the answer. "The Lord is my light and my salvation—whom shall I fear? The Lord is the stronghold of my life—of whom shall I be afraid" (Psalm 27:1)? His response was, "I will not fear though tens of thousands assail me on every side" (Psalm 3:6).

We shouldn't be discouraged, because nothing new is going on here. As Solomon wrote, "What has been will be again, what has been done will be done again; there is nothing new under the sun. Is there anything one can see or hear and say, 'Look! This is something new?' It was here already, long ago. It was here before our time" (Ecclesiastes 1:9–10). God turned the lives of Noah and his family upside down when he decided to wipe humankind off the face of the earth. Jesus rerouted the lives of twelve ordinary men toward a completely new destination, changing the course of their lives and the world. Jesus put Saul face down on a dusty road and changed his life as well as the lives of Gentiles. These people faced huge, immediate changes in their lives. God isn't calling us to do anything other flawed humans haven't already done, nor is he necessarily calling us to be changed immediately, but he is calling us, today, to decide the path we will take and to begin our journey.

Satan encourages chaos because he knows it produces fear. Fear generates doubt and weakness. When fear and doubt are present for a prolonged period, they can foster despair, resulting in paralysis followed by surrender, if left uncorrected. On the other hand, fear can also produce vulnerability, resulting in some soul-searching questions and a desire to be rescued. Most of us have observed this soul searching firsthand. At the funeral of a family member, I overheard my uncle questioning Dad regarding how to enter heaven and if the deceased relative was going to heaven. Clearly, the family member's death had prompted these questions regarding eternity. On another occasion, I received a phone call from a relative. He was outside and had seen the moon, large and low in the sky and appearing very red to him. He was concerned because he remembered a passage in the Bible stating the moon would turn blood red near the end of time, and he was wondering if he needed to "do something" before the end came. More opportunities to address eternal matters will likely come our way as the chaos and violence continue and intensify.

I watched a lot of television on September 11, 2001, and over the following days. Hopelessness was one of the most prevalent conditions being expressed by the witnesses. However, over time the hopelessness seemed to lessen.

In August 2006, the Barna Group released an article entitled, "Five Years Later: 9/11 Attacks Show No Lasting Influence on Americans' Faith," which stated,

> In the immediate aftermath of the attacks, half of all Americans said their faith helped them cope with the shock and uncertainty. The change most widely reported was a significant spike in church attendance, with some churches experiencing more than double their normal crowd on the Sunday after the shocking event. However, by the time January 2002 rolled around, churchgoing was

back to pre-attack levels, and has remained consistent in the five years since.[2]

During the week of May 16, 2011, I was teaching a class in California. A full-page ad appeared in a national newspaper announcing judgment day would begin that week with a worldwide earthquake. There was some lively classroom discussion the day the advertisement appeared, mostly banter regarding the end times. There was also more somber conversation that evening after class as questions were posed and pondered. Several media articles, published after the world did not end, recounted individual supporters of that belief who had quit jobs or spent their life savings to advertise the impending apocalypse.

The two occurrences, one real and one predicted, were traumatic, one-time events resulting in some short-lived soul searching. I see one significant difference in our circumstance today. The chaos, violence, and division we are experiencing is not a one-time event but a continuing pattern of increasing intensity. I believe this is true because the nature of the changes is ideological, representing long-term, if not permanent, effects on our society.

It seems United States Attorney General William Barr may have drawn a similar conclusion. According to a Justice News release on October 11, 2019, Barr spoke at the law school at Notre Dame University stating,

> Now, there have been times and places where the traditional moral order has been shaken. In the past, societies—like the human body—seem to have a self-healing mechanism—a self-correcting mechanism that gets things back on course if things go too far . . . This is the idea of the pendulum. We have all thought that after a while the "pendulum will swing back." But today we face something different that may mean that we cannot count on the pendulum swinging back. First is the force, fervor, and comprehensiveness of the assault on religion we are experiencing today. This is not decay; it is organized destruction.[3]

Consider some of the decades-long battles, mentioned earlier, that are fundamental to the societal changes we see today.

- The number of people who profess faith in Christ, Bible knowledge, and church attendance has been decreasing with each generation.
- Self-centeredness has been increasing with each generation.
- Desperation and hopelessness are increasing, as evidenced by increased depression, drug use, and suicide.
- The family unit is disintegrating and has taken on many new variations.
- God's definition of marriage has been tossed out by the US government, replaced by humankind's definition.
- The sanctity of life is eroding more and more as time passes.
- Random violence and lawlessness have been increasing for years.
- Islamic extremism against Christianity will last as long Islamic extremists live.
- Those in America who desire an alternate lifestyle will not be satisfied until every detractor is silenced.

As Dr. Albert Mohler states in his book, *The Gathering Storm*,

> The LGBTQ revolution demands not only equality but also the suppression of divergent worldviews, namely, the Christian worldview. Any moral code that denies their new sexual rights must be silenced, for, in (Moises) Kaufman's words, the worldview is nothing more than the vestige of an authoritarian system of oppression. These words come not as friendly debate and discourse over moral issues—they are the words of revolution, and a revolution seeking nothing less than unconditional surrender from its enemies.[4]

For these reasons and others, many people in America are scared today. As I walked through the grocery store during the 2020 coronavirus pandemic, many faces were covered by masks to prevent the spread of the virus. However, I could see everyone's eyes, and many of them held fear. People needed to shop for groceries, but they didn't want to be in the store because they feared becoming infected. The coronavirus pandemic, while a scary change, is temporary, but I don't think the virus is the entire reason for the fear in the eyes of Americans. Long-standing moral norms are being discarded. This fosters troubling questions, like what comes next? Where are we headed? What will happen to me? Living in a state of fear is a horrible plight, but I believe it will generate significant soul searching among our fellow citizens. For some, this will result in a positive eternal outcome.

Gary Inrig makes timely, accurate observations about twenty-first century Christians navigating life in these rapidly changing times. In his book, *True North*, Gary compares Christians to seafarers, attempting to navigate the turbulent waters of life. Here are a few quotes.

- "We are living in uncharted territory. The familiar land-marks have vanished, and the old cultural maps are outdated. So, we need to think not so much of maps as of navigational skills, not so much of travel guides as of principles which will help us find our way through the fluid, complex, fast-changing ocean on which we have to navigate."[5]
- "The Bible is the Christian's sextant. It takes the fixed point of the triune God, the North Star, and brings it down to the horizon to locate us in time and space."[6]
- "The Lord Jesus Christ . . . is the fixed point, the North Star. He is the indispensable constant to enable us to live life well. If He is not the fixed reference point by which we constantly determine our location and direction, we are doomed to flounder."[6]

Christians are unique because they are persecuted for their faith in Jesus. Christians in our homeland today have another unique distinction. We have been given the opportunity to present the gospel to a growing segment of Americans who are either scripturally illiterate or nearly so. The Bible tells us that the world will get darker as time passes. God's Spirit has been preparing us, training us to respond appropriately in these last days, and God gave us the perfect solution for this dark world. He wants us to let the light of Jesus Christ shine bright through us. Then some of those who are groping about in the darkness will be drawn to his light. The saved and the lost need calm mariners, seasoned by the storms of life, to help navigate everyone safely to the final shore.

A Uniquely Qualified Group

Let's continue with Gary Inrig's seafarer analogy for a moment.

- What humans are best qualified to pilot the Body of Christ through the uncharted turbulent waters of America today?
- What humans are best equipped to help lost souls navigate the dire straits of chaos, hate, and fear?
- I would propose one answer: the most experienced mariners who have been utilizing the North Star (Jesus) and the sextant (the Bible) to navigate life for decades.

I am convinced our elder ambassadors of the kingdom of heaven are the most well-equipped group of believers to lead the Body of Christ through our changing times in America, to serve as the boatswains or quartermasters, if you will. This same group of Christians is also the most well-equipped group of believers to lead lost souls through the storms of life by pointing them to Jesus Christ, to serve as spiritual lighthouse keepers. Three points of clarification need to be made here.

- These elder ambassadors are, by my definition, those who continually seek and follow the leading of the Holy Spirit in all things.
- Singling out the elder ambassadors is not meant to impugn the faithfulness, skills, or godly desires of younger or newer Christians in any way.
- Scripture is clear. The entire Body of Christ is called to present the gospel to the world.

What characteristics or traits set these elder ambassadors apart from the rest of the Body of Christ? The have devoted decades to:

- Building an intimate relationship with God Almighty and his Son, Jesus Christ.
- Internalizing God's Word through study and memorization, knowing it is the truth. Through their experience they have seen God's promises never fail.

- Understanding and recalling Scripture. If, someday, all the Bibles were removed from America, they would be able to correctly convey, from memory, the basics of God's Word to anyone who would listen.
- Applying God's Word to their lives daily. They have attempted to live according to Scripture, serving faithfully, making sacrifices to help advance the kingdom of heaven, and befriending those in need.
- Experiencing the working of the Holy Spirit in their lives. Their faith has increased when the Spirit has shown them some victories for their efforts.
- Being humbled by the disappointments, suffering, trials, and defeats that come from living with a sinful nature in a sinful world.
- Gaining empathy for lost souls. They understand lost souls because they were lost once themselves.
- Serving those in need because Jesus Christ served them in their greatest need.
- Exhibiting true peace and joy despite life's heartaches, a joy only produced by faith in Jesus Christ as Lord and Savior.
- Perfecting their love as parents and grandparents toward their children and grandchildren.
- Honing one-on-one communication skills to develop relationships.
- Investing time in relationships with other people, designed to produce an eternal result.
- Persevering in an unshakable faith in God Almighty and Jesus Christ no matter what life may bring.

From my perspective, such people have a PhD in Christian living. This very minute men, women, young, old, Black, White, rich, poor, educated, uneducated, saved, and lost are confused and searching for answers to questions with eternal implications. These people, some of whom are our relatives, friends, and fellow Americans, are seeking:

- The truth—They live in a society where truth is relative. Absolute right and wrong don't exist. If only they had a friend who would share the truth of Christ with them.
- Purpose—If they can't find the truth, how can they find their true purpose in life? How can they plot a course allowing them to make a

significant contribution to humankind? If only they had a friend who would share God's purpose for their life.
- Peace—They live in a country, and a world, where peace is a rare commodity, where chaos, strife, and war are the norm, and where uncertainty is the order of the day. If only they had a friend who would share the source of true peace with them.
- Freedom—They live in a world shackled by the slavery of sin. If only they had a friend, one who has fought the battles against sin and persevered (however imperfectly) to share the freedom that comes by living for Christ.
- Love—They live in a time when hatred and apathy are in vogue, where the essence of love has been perverted or abandoned. If only they had a friend who would love them as Jesus loves them.
- Hope—Our world is fresh out of hope. If only they had a friend who possessed true hope, one who would be willing to point them to the source of hope.

The relationship between grandparents and grandchildren is special because their love is unique. These elders only have the best interest of their grandchildren at heart, and the grandchildren know this because of the love they are shown. Therefore, when grandparents speak, grandchildren usually listen and believe. Likewise, you, as elder ambassadors for the kingdom of heaven, are the ones who can look "seekers" in the eye and tell them the truth in love, just as grandparents talk to their grandchildren. As you tell them what the Lord Jesus Christ has done for you, a sinner just like them, they will find no condemnation in you because decades of life with many failures along the way has produced humility in you. They will see no arrogance in your eyes or hear any doubt in your words because love is motivating the words given to you by the Holy Spirit. They may or may not accept your Savior, but they will listen to and consider what you have to say. Because of your life in Christ, God wants to give you these opportunities.

I am convinced God has placed us where we are for such a time as this (Esther 4:14) to set us in the path of people who are seeking the truth or who are open to the truth. They desire something else in their lives, even if they can't specifically identify it. Every believer can address the needs and desires of lost souls because their needs and desires can be wrapped up in four words: "Hope through the truth." Today is the day, and this is the hour for our elder ambassadors to exert influence to counter the gathering darkness. I don't mean by standing on street corners holding signs or protesting our godless government. I mean by developing one-on-one relationships with those who are willing to get to know you. Then, in time, they may give you an opportunity for you to tell them the reason for your hope. They will want to understand how you can exhibit true peace and joy in a chaotic world.

As our elder ambassadors take the lead in reaching out to the lost world, some of the younger ambassadors will come alongside them. They will want to learn, to follow the leadership of those more experienced, to grow in their walk with Christ through service, and to share their witness with the world. How do I know? Do you remember the twenty thousand Christian college students who told Francis Chan there was something missing in their spiritual lives?[8] Many more than twenty thousand young believers have a strong desire to impact their world for the kingdom of God. Our role is exquisitely simple. Love people one-on-one until they understand you love them. Then point them to Jesus Christ and tell them that Jesus loves them too.

One final word on our adequacy or lack thereof: it's not about us. It's all about him. In our human strength, we are completely inadequate, but as Christians indwelt by God's Spirit, we can accomplish anything within God's will. God can use anyone or anything he chooses to convey his message. He has proven it to humans before. If God can speak to Balaam through a donkey (Numbers 22:28–31), he can speak to another human through me and you.

A Living Hope

I've never met a person who said, "I don't want to have hope. I'd rather live without it." We don't have to be Rhodes scholars to understand such a concept is preposterous on its face. We all have desires that we sincerely hope will be realized: a happy marriage, a healthy family, friends who truly love us. Life would be dark and dreary without it because despair is the opposite of hope. Despair, like an invisible virulent flu, is a spiritual disease spreading through America, infecting more of our population each day. An axiom found in various forms on the Internet regarding Christians says something like this: "We do not have a hopeless end but an endless hope." Our endless hope is also a present, living hope through the resurrection of Jesus Christ.

Therefore, my message to the world is "hope through the truth." Our hope is in God's Word, the eternal, flawless truth. Our God, who is all-powerful and unchanging, has promised us eternal life if we have faith in the crucified, resurrected Jesus Christ as our Lord and Savior (1 Peter 3:15, 18). God will deliver on his certain promise in his own good time. Conversely, worldly hope is nothing more than an unlikely wish, such as winning the lottery this month. Is it possible? Yes, but what are the odds? Such wishes have virtually no chance of occurring. Some worldly hopes do have a reasonable, or even probable, chance of coming true. Still, such hopes are temporary at best, going to the grave with us. Lost souls who understand that eternity exists hope everyone goes to heaven. Those who don't believe in eternity, heaven, or hell only have temporary wishes in this life. Those who are without faith in Jesus Christ have no eternal hope.

As we journey through life, we will encounter people who will propose various theories regarding our origin, God, and eternity. Some non-believers may say what Christians call a "living hope" is just a fairy tale, devoid of any credible evidence to support such a claim and outside the realm of possibility. To such people I say, "When I understand the marvelously intricate complexities of the human body, the unequaled beauty of our earth, the unimaginable vastness of our universe, and how all these are perfectly interconnected to support human life on earth, I can only conclude all of this was created by a God whose knowledge is incomprehensible to me. Furthermore, I find it unfathomable even to consider that all this took place by chance." In my mind, the odds of evolution resulting in our universe as it is today are so infinitesimally small that they are a practical impossibility.

Others may say God doesn't exist, all paths lead to God, or when we die, everything ends. If these statements are true, then let's eat, drink, and be merry. Some may ask, "What if there is no God? What if death on earth is the end of us?" I would respond, "If I live my life as God commands, when I die, I will leave this world a better place. While alive I will have tried to be a good citizen, to help those in need, and to treat everyone with love." Then I would ask, "But what if I'm right, and you are wrong? What happens to you after you die and are then raised to answer to God for your life on earth if there is an eternal heaven and eternal torment?"

I am convinced somewhere deep within our souls that every human comprehends the existence of an Almighty God who wants us to seek, find, and know us. A person may try to suppress or deny this truth, but the existence of the truth cannot be negated. Scripture tells us God "set eternity in the human heart; yet no one can fathom what God has done from beginning to end" (Ecclesiastes 3:11). Why would God set eternity in our hearts if eternity doesn't exist? Scripture tells us God made us, so we "would seek him and perhaps reach out for him and find him" (Acts 17:26–27). God wouldn't build into us a desire to seek something or someone that doesn't exist. Randy Allen, senior minister at Bethel Church of Christ in Ada, Ohio, while preaching on Ecclesiastes 3, said, "God gives us the truth about human existence. God created you and he has not put any desires in your heart that cannot be fulfilled. We have been made for something more. We were created by God for eternity."

We also have practical earthly evidence, in addition to the Bible, proving that humankind intuitively knows God exists. Most of us are familiar with stories about an unsaved soul who is suddenly faced with impending death or catastrophic injury and calls out to God for help, a sincere, frantic call. As the proverb says, "There are no atheists in foxholes." Furtive prayers of lost souls are evidence that humankind believes God exists no matter what people proclaim. Driving a vehicle on the roads in Sicily is not for the faint of heart. Those native to the home of Ferrari, Lamborghini, and Alfa Romeo seem to consider themselves bona fide world-class race car drivers. There weren't many good, paved roads in Sicily when I was there and even fewer straight roads. So, any stretch of straight road brought out the racer in every Sicilian driver. Stoplights in the few sizable cities were not the law; they were a suggestion. Stop signs were, for the most part, ignored. In two years, I never saw anyone pulled over for speeding.

I was driving home from the naval base one evening, and Susie was in the car with me. The turn into the community where we lived was made from a nice stretch of flat four-lane paved road. I had to cross oncoming traffic to make the turn. I slowed down in the passing lane to make the turn onto a dirt road leading to the house I was renting. I always engaged the turn signal well ahead of this stop. The lane directly behind me was clear, but the right-hand lane was full as everyone was moving over to pass me on the right. The two lanes of oncoming traffic were packed with traffic as well. I waited for any break in traffic to make the turn.

When I glanced into the rear-view mirror, I discovered a horrible sight. A vehicle was bearing down on us at an enormous rate of speed. The vehicle's headlights filled the rear-view mirror, and there was no way he was going to be able to stop. We were a few seconds from a crash. The thought would have made me sick if I would have had a chance to think about it. (Later, I did think about it—a lot.) Susie didn't know what was happening because she couldn't see what I saw in the rear-view mirror, but she understood something bad was about to happen when I leaned over, pulled her toward me, and said, "God help us!" It was no flippant remark, using the Lord's name casually or taking it in vain. It was one of the shortest and certainly one of the most fervent prayers I have ever uttered. And God did help us!

Susie and I were sitting in the front seat of the car, leaning toward each other with our heads touching. I couldn't see through the rear-view mirror from that position as the approaching car reached our position. A moment later my car shook violently as the vehicle screamed past, inches away from the driver's side of my car. Because the driver had passed on my left, his vehicle was now hurtling in the wrong direction—in the passing lane of oncoming traffic. So, the drivers in the passing lane had to swerve to avoid him. Each of these turns made by many drivers resulted in oncoming traffic passing our car on the right and the left while traffic coming up behind our car in our direction were doing the same thing.

It was surreal. It was like one of those cartoons I've seen where a hundred cars are driving in all four directions through an intersection at breakneck speed, weaving past each other, yet no one wrecks. However, this was no cartoon, and it was mortifying. I can't begin to tell you how many cars passed our car while we sat in the middle of the four-lane road. At the end of it, we made the left-hand turn onto the dirt road leading to our house. Not one car had hit another car. Not one car had wrecked by driving off the road into the fields. It was literally impossible for what I saw to have happened, but it did. I mentioned earlier that I should have died several times while I was lost. That was one of those times.

Funerals are another piece of practical earthly evidence that God exists. Have you noticed the difference between a funeral for a Christian and a funeral for a lost soul? The loss of a loved one carries so much sorrow with it, whether the deceased is saved or lost. However, when I grieve the death of a loved one who is a Christian, my grief is for me. The world is a lesser place for me when someone I love dies, but the grief is slightly lessened because I know the separation is temporary; we will be reunited. I have a biblical hope of a reunion, an assurance founded in eternity on God's covenant. I can't wait to see Mom and Dad again. Knowing their spirits are in God's hands makes heaven even better for me (I know this is purely human thinking). However, those who are grieving the loss of an unsaved soul suffer an eternal loss. Their sadness is inconsolable. Their grief is distinctly different, as those who have no hope because, in fact, they have no hope for the deceased.

I would like to offer one final piece of practical earthly evidence of God. Is there a significant difference in how Christians and non-believers deal with their own deaths? If I have no idea where I am going or what comes after death, if anything, death produces anxiety and fear of the unknown. For believers, this current stage of life is preparation for the next stage. After all, for Christians, life on earth is simply a dress rehearsal for eternity.

A little more than two years after Mom died, Dad was diagnosed with a virulent form of cancer in the spring of 2015. I'll never forget the first and only appointment Dad had with his oncologist. After a minute of pleasantries, the doctor said, "Mr. Holstein, I have bad news for you. You have cancer."

"OK," Dad replied.

"Mr. Holstein, this particular type of cancer is very aggressive," the doctor continued.

"Really?" Dad said. He didn't appear to be upset. Instead, he seemed calm, almost nonchalant. These two could have been talking about the weather. It was obvious the doctor was caught off guard by Dad's demeanor, but he continued, talking in some detail about Dad's particular form of cancer and the specific chemotherapy regimen he recommended for treatment.

I had two questions for the doctor. What was the prognosis for life expectancy with the chemotherapy and without the chemotherapy? The doctor gave the same response to both questions, "Weeks or months but not years." Then he asked Dad when he wanted to start the chemotherapy, urging sooner rather than later. Dad said he would have to get back with the doctor, who was thoroughly perplexed. "Mr. Holstein, do you understand what I'm saying to you? You have a virulent form of cancer, and you are dying."

"Yes. I'll get back with you," Dad said. Then we left the doctor's office.

"The doctor can't do anything for me," Dad said on the car ride back to the house. I agreed. Dad knew only God could change his circumstance. Dad told me he wasn't taking any chemotherapy, and he was going to stay in his house until the Lord called him home. That's exactly what he did. My brother, my sister, my wife, Susie (who is a retired registered nurse), and hospice took care of Dad until he died.

Mom and Dad had been married sixty-four years. She had significant health issues for many years. Their common prayer had been the Lord would take Mom home before Dad, so Dad could take care of Mom here on earth.

God granted their request. What the oncologist didn't understand was Dad did not fear death. He knew who was in control. He was ready for the Lord to call him home. Dad knew what was next, where he was going, and that he would be with Mom again. Dad had a good life on earth. He pointed quite a few souls to Jesus Christ. Dad's demeanor in his final weeks showed his faith was rock solid. Those who saw him near the end knew it too. God was most gracious, as he usually is, and took Dad out on a high note.

When Dad pastored in Hugheston, West Virginia, he also served as a mentor to a younger man, Gary, who wanted to be a pastor. After Dad visited with his oncologist, Gary showed up at dad's house one day. I sat outside the bedroom door and listened as the two of them talked for several hours. One of the stories was about when Dad left Hugheston. Gary stepped in as the interim pastor. Fifty years later, Gary is still the "interim" pastor at that little church in Hugheston. Dad and Gary had a good laugh about that. They had many stories to tell each other, and both of them relished the moment, reminiscing as they recounted their numerous adventures together in Christ. It was one dear brother in Christ telling the other not "Goodbye" but rather "I'll see you later."

When Gary left, Dad took to his bed and never got out of it again. A couple of days later, Dad went to his eternal home. When my time comes, I want to finish the way Dad did, with rock-solid assurance that I loved the Lord, worked hard to impact the kingdom of heaven here on earth, and with a certain knowledge the best is yet to come.

One day I will stand before the Lord and give an account for my sins, whether by omission or commission. To be sure, I am not questioning my salvation because I am covered by the blood of Jesus. Hopefully, both types of sins are decreasing in my life rather than increasing as I gain experience in my walk with the Lord. When I do come face to face with the Lord, I don't want to feel regret about what I could have done or should have done. I want to finish strong, as much as I am able. For those who have no interest in God's plan of salvation or Jesus Christ, I have no desire to bore them with my story. The short time I have left must be used wisely. While I am still here, I want the opportunity to address anyone who wants to hear. I would like to remind Christians of the hope we have in Jesus and encourage them in their walk with him. I would like to tell non-Christians what Jesus Christ has done for me, to point them to him. I would like to tell lost souls who are seeking the truth the reason for the hope within me. I am convinced the field is still ripe for harvest in America. Every believer knows how to tell the truth. More than ever before in my lifetime, America needs people who are willing to share the light, salt, and truth of the gospel message. Therein lies the hope for our families, friends, and fellow citizens. Jesus's plan for believers making disciples of all nations has been the same, straightforward method he modeled two thousand years ago. It has not changed one iota.

Whether it is a large crowd, a small group, or one person who is willing to listen, tell people the good news of the kingdom of heaven and how it has changed your life. We honor God by stating the truth in love with humility, by praying for the Holy Spirit to convict the lost, and by asking the Lord to provide opportunities to witness. Whether or not anyone ever accepts the gospel message they hear from us, we still honor God through these endeavors. His "marching orders" are simple enough for every soldier in his army to understand and employ. God wants us to point everyone who will listen to Jesus Christ, utilizing our personal testimony. In this manner we can become God's instruments of change in our country, one soul at a time. Our families, friends, and neighbors need to hear this message more than ever.

Conclusion

In these pages, we have considered three fundamental, interconnected questions.

- Is something significant missing from my spiritual life?
- What is my purpose in life?
- What is truth?

Only you can answer these questions for yourself. Your answers to these three questions will shape everything you do and how you do it. However, you need to consider these questions in reverse order to arrive at the correct responses.

- First, we need to determine what the truth is and then apply it to the other two questions. For me, the inerrant truth is God's Word, the Holy Bible, embodied by Jesus Christ as he walked this earth and provided the perfect example of how we should live. Any source that contradicts Scripture is false.
- Second, based on the truth, God's Word, it is crystal clear that our singular purpose in life is to bring glory to God in everything we say and do in the name of Jesus Christ, our Lord and Savior.
- Only then can we answer the first question in this book. As for me, yes, something is missing from my spiritual life. I need to have a more intimate relationship with Jesus. One of the ways I can contribute more to this relationship is to wait expectantly and excitedly for those opportunities the Holy Spirit will provide, so I can impact someone here on earth for the kingdom of heaven.

CONCLUSION

As I said early on, God has blessed me throughout my life. I believe one of the reasons for these blessings is because I have been such a needy person my entire life.

- As a child, I needed a godly mother and father to give me my foundation in Christ. So, God blessed me with them.
- As a young man who was lost, I needed godly men and women who would befriend me and model the example of a Christlike life. So, God blessed me with such people.
- As a young Christian, I needed godly men and women who would teach me the Word, give me sound advice for daily living, and encourage me on my new journey through life. So, God blessed me with such people.
- Today, I need godly men and women to help me through the daily struggles of life and come alongside me to help me in my walk with the Lord. So, God continues to bless me with such people.
- All my life, I have needed to be loved and accepted. So, God continually shows me his love and acceptance. He has also provided me with several humans who show me unconditional love and acceptance.
- All my life, I have needed to be considered important to someone, to have added something of value to the world around me. So, God continues to show me his plan for my life. Even more, he has shown me that my value to him is beyond words. How do I know this? Because Jesus Christ died for me.

God has met my needs every day.

- When I was a lost soul, God used Christians who stood in the breach between my gutter of sin and his offer of eternal life, encouraging and guiding me out of the gutter and pointing me toward Jesus Christ.
- As a saved soul, God has used believers to help me when I have struggled in my walk with Christ.

God Almighty has always operated this way. Throughout history, he has been watching everything we do all the time (Psalm 33:13). As God has observed us, he has always been searching for a particular person or persons, those who want to understand him (Psalm 14:2). It has always been God's desire for someone to "stand in the gap" for him, bridging the gap that separates lost souls from eternal life with God. Mind you, God desires, but does not need, humans to serve in this role. God is fully able to achieve his plan and has acted alone for this purpose when no humans were willing to work with him.

- On one occasion, the Lord, speaking through Ezekiel said, "I looked for someone among them who would build up the wall and stand before me in the gap on behalf of the land so I would not have to destroy it, but I found no one. So, I will pour out my wrath on them and consume them with my fiery anger" (Ezekiel 22:30–31).
- Another time, the Lord, speaking through Isaiah said, "The Lord looked and was displeased that there was no justice. He saw that there was no one, he was appalled that there was no one to intervene; so, his own arm achieved salvation for him, and his own righteousness sustained him" (Isaiah 59:15–16).

On several other occasions, God waited quite a while for someone to come forward in his name.

- When the Philistine and Israelite armies gathered for battle, Goliath, the Philistine champion, came forward every morning and evening to challenge any Israelite to face him in battle. This went on for forty days because no Israelite was willing to fight him, until a young shepherd, named David, challenged Goliath. David, incensed that a heathen would slander his God, slew Goliath with a sling and a single stone by the power of the Holy Spirit (I Samuel 17:48–50).
- At one point in time, the Lord prophesied against the shepherds of Israel through the prophet Ezekiel because they did not care for the flock. They didn't strengthen the weak or bind up the injured sheep. They didn't even search for the sheep who went astray but left them to the wild animals. Therefore, the Lord declared, "because my flock lacks a shepherd . . . I will rescue my flock . . . I will search for my sheep and look after them . . . I will search for the lost and bring back the strays" (Ezekiel 34:10–16).

At other times, God did not have to wait for someone to stand in the gap for him.

- Abraham stood in the gap for God by interceding on behalf of the cities of Sodom and Gomorrah, asking that they be spared from annihilation (Genesis 18:20–26).
- Moses stood in the breach between a sinful people and a holy God by interceding on behalf of Israel with prayers of forgiveness and healing (Psalm 106:23).
- Esther stood in the gap by interceding on behalf of the Jews in captivity in Persia when she went to King Xerxes to beg for the Jews to be spared from annihilation (Esther 8:3–6).

I am convinced of three timeless truths. Every day:

- God is looking for someone who will stand in the gap, to stand in the breach for him.
- God is calling me to act within his will.
- It is my turn to help others, as so many have helped me in the past.

When I repented of my sins, and God placed his Holy Spirit within me, I was no longer the needy person I used to be. Don't get me wrong; I am still a needy person, but God empowered me by his Spirit. From the day I gave my life to the Lord, I've had something I can give back, and God expects me to give it back. Throughout these pages I have included the names of some of the Christians who have helped in my conversion to Christ and my growth as a believer. Those names are here to show you the large amount of human resources God was willing to utilize to save one lost soul: mine. Those names are also here as proof that God uses normal, flawed believers every day to eternally impact the kingdom of heaven. God expects me to get out there into the world and be a help to others.

As a youngster, I loved roller coasters. I grew up riding those rickety wooden roller coasters that would shake, rattle, and roll the brains around in my head. Growing up in Charleston, West Virginia, we had one amusement park to go to unless we wanted to make a trip out of state. Camden Park, near Huntington, West Virginia, had a wooden roller coaster called the Big Dipper. I have ridden it more times than any other roller coaster. Sometimes our family would take a trip to Cincinnati, Ohio. We would always visit Kings Island, home of the Beast, once billed as the longest wooden roller coaster in the world. Then there was Space Mountain at Disneyworld's Magic Kingdom in Orlando, Florida. It was no wooden coaster; it was a dark, indoor, high-speed outer-space-themed roller coaster. What made Space Mountain significantly different from the wooden roller coasters I had experienced was the darkness. I couldn't see my hand in front of my face, much less the next dip or turn in the track. I didn't know what was coming next. I haven't been on a roller coaster in years, but I remember the exhilaration of those rides like it was yesterday. It was, in a word, "thrilling."

As we grow older, trips to the amusement park are replaced with trips to the grocery store, commuting to and from work, chores at home, cutting the grass (or shoveling the snow), and paying the bills. Grown-up life can be, in a word, "boring." It's no wonder companies profit by reintroducing exhilaration into adult lives. They offer many activities, including hot-air ballooning, helicopter rides, skydiving, whitewater rafting, zipline tours, exotic supercar driving, mountain climbing, and nature watching among others.

I get it. Working for a living, raising a family, and paying bills is not as exciting as a day at the amusement park. Most adults would probably like a little more adventure in their lives. But life for adults doesn't have to be boring. In fact, the life of a Christian should be anything but boring. God has called those who believe in Jesus Christ as Lord and Savior to be his heralds, his ambassadors. God created many different roles within the Body of Christ, provided a variety of different spiritual gifts to Christians, and planned specific tasks to be completed by humans because he wants to use us in a mighty way to further his kingdom. God wants us to be willing workers in this endeavor. However, God's plan does not *require* our participation for at least three reasons.

First, God is all-powerful and can achieve his goals in his own power without help from anyone. Second, God's plan is guaranteed to succeed with or without human help. Speaking through Isaiah, God said, "I looked, but there was no one to help. I was appalled that no one gave support. So, my own arm achieved salvation for me, and my own wrath sustained me" (Isaiah 63:5). As the Psalmist tells us, "But the plans of the Lord stand firm forever" (Psalm 33:11). Third, God has a non-human witness called creation. The Psalmist writes, "The heavens declare the glory of God; the skies proclaim the work of his hands. Day after day they pour forth speech; night after night they reveal knowledge. They have no speech; they use no words; no sound is heard from them. Yet their voice goes out into all the earth, their words to the ends of the world" (Psalm 19:1–4). Jesus addressed creation as a witness also. When the Pharisees told Jesus to rebuke his disciples for praising him, Jesus replied, "I tell you if they keep quiet, the stones will cry out" (Luke 19:40).

I grew up in an era when young kids in the neighborhood played outside all the time (weather and parents permitting). We would make up role-playing games like "cops and robbers" or "cowboys and Indians." One time I would be the cop, and another time I would be the robber, but I always wanted to be the good guy, the knight in shining armor, the hero in the story. Though I didn't understand it at the time, this role-playing allowed me to experience a deep-seated need in my psyche, a need to be important to someone, to have added something of value to the world around me. As I achieved that goal through role-playing, I also led a thrilling life as the "victor." What I pretended through role-playing as a child, God desired me to experience in real life as an adult with the Holy Spirit's help.

Engaging in sin may seem a lot of "fun," but it is a life of drudgery because it is fraught with guilt, shame, pain, and anxiety. But the worst outcome of such a lifestyle is yet to come, a horrible, pitiless eternity of indescribable torment. God has no desire for anyone to have such a destiny. In fact, the opposite is true. God wants to take us on a journey where we will encounter opportunities to impact eternal destinies at every turn, a journey as exhilarating for us as it is beneficial to the kingdom of heaven. God wants us to be more than excited. He wants us to be ecstatic every day as we anticipate, not knowing what will happen next. He wants us to wait with bated breath for every opportunity he provides. He wants us to look back at the end of our lives and say with all sincerity, "Wow. What a ride. Thank you, God, for taking me on such an adventure. I held onto you as best I could." That is the "full life" Jesus told us he came to bring us (John 10:10).

I am reminded of a sinful human who enthusiastically responded to God's offer. By that choice, his life was changed forever. When the Lord Almighty revealed himself in a vision, Isaiah was devastated by his uncleanness in the presence of perfect holiness. Immediately, he knew he was a filthy, spiritually bankrupt person compared to the perfect, Almighty God. Like Isaiah, we are all unclean, spiritually bankrupt people. Once God had revealed himself, he posed two direct questions: "Whom shall I send?" and "Who will go for us?" God knew in advance how Isaiah would respond, but Isaiah didn't know until he heard the questions. The decision was left to Isaiah (Isaiah 6:1–8). You know the rest of the story.

I like Oswald Chambers' observations regarding this passage of Scripture. In his book, *My Utmost for His Highest,* he says, "God did not address the call to Isaiah; Isaiah overheard God saying, 'Who will go for us?' The call of God is not for the special few, it is for everyone . . . If we let the Spirit of God bring us face to face with God, we too shall hear something akin to what Isaiah heard, the still small voice of God; and in perfect freedom will say, 'Here am I; send me'."[1]

Precious souls hang in the balance. Jesus is asking you, "Will you answer the call?"

If you do answer the call, you will never again have to ask, "Is something significant missing from my spiritual life?" It's between you and God, no one else. It's personal!

Notes

Chapter 1—A Blessed Life

1. Francis Chan, *Crazy Love* (Colorado Springs, CO: David C. Cook, 2008), 179.
2. Ibid., 7.

Chapter 2—Our Purpose

1. Centers for Disease Control and Prevention, National Center for Health Statistics, "Table 44. Personal health care expenditures, by source of funds and type of expenditure: United States, selected years 1960–2017," last viewed October 27, 2020, https://www.cdc.gov/nchs/data/hus/2018/044.pdf, 4.
2. National Institute of Mental Health, "Major Depression," February 2019, https://www.nimh.nih.gov/health/statistics/major-depression.shtml, 2, 5.
3. Lisa J. Colpe, PhD, MPH, "Deaths of Despair: How Connecting Opioid Data Extends the Possibilities for Suicide Research," Centers for Disease Control and Prevention, April 2, 2020, https://www.cdc.gov/surveillance/blogs-stories/deaths-of-dispair.html.
4. Gary Inrig, *True North—Discovering God's Way in a Changing World* (Grand Rapids, MI: Discovery House Publishers, 2002), 105.
5. Francis Chan, *Crazy Love* (Colorado Springs, CO: David C. Cook, 2008), 19.
6. Bob Briner, *Roaring Lambs: A Gentle Plan to Radically Change Your World* (Grand Rapids, MI: Zondervan, 1993), 15.
7. Ibid., 18.
8. Ibid., 21.

9   Richard Warren, *The Purpose-Driven Life* (Grand Rapids, MI: Zondervan, 2002), 3.
10 Ibid., 7-8.

Chapter 5—The Struggle Against Self

1   Pew Research Center, "Baby Boomers: The Gloomiest Generation," June 25, 2008, https://www.pewsocialtrends.org/2008/06/25/baby-boomers-the-gloomiest-generation/.
2   Paul Taylor, "More Than Half of Millennials Have Shared a 'Selfie,'" Pew Research Center, March 4, 2014, https://www.pewresearch.org/fact-tank/2014/03/04/more-than-half-of-millennials-have-shared-a-selfie/.
3   Amanda Barrosa, Kim Parker and Jesse Bennett, "As Millennials Near 40, They're Approaching Family Life Differently Than Previous Generations," Pew Research Center, May 27, 2020, https://www.pewsocialtrends.org/2020/05/27/as-millennials-near-40-theyre-approaching-family-life-differently-than-previous-generations/.
4   Brett & Kate McKay, "The Eisenhower Decision Matrix: How to Distinguish Between Urgent and Important Tasks and Make Real Progress in Your Life," Art of Manliness, last updated September 19, 2020, https://www.artofmanliness.com/articles/eisenhower-decision-matrix/.

Chapter 6—The Struggle with the Word of God

1   Barna Group, "The End of Absolutes: America's New Moral Code," May 25, 2016, https://www.barna.com/research/the-end-of-absolutes-americas-new-moral-code/.

Chapter 7—The Struggle with Servanthood

1   Circle of Hope, "Saints and Holy Days We Want to Remember—Clara McBride," December 18, 2018, https://www.circleofhope.net/transhistorical/december-18-clara-mcbride-hale/.
2   Child Evangelism Fellowship, "Our History," last viewed November 15, 2020, https://www.cefonline.com/about/history/.
3   Stu Weber, *Tender Warrior* (Sisters, OR: Multnomah Books, 1993), 14.
4   Brian Jones, *Hell is Real (But I Hate to Admit It)* (Colorado Springs, CO: David C. Cook, 2011), 48.
5   Ibid., 49.

NOTES

Chapter 8—The Struggle Against Flesh and Blood

1. Congressional Research Service, "American War and Military Operations Casualties: Lists and Statistics," Table I, Federation of American Scientists, July 29, 2020, https://fas.org/sgp/crs/natsec/RL32492.pdf.
2. National Archives and Records Administration, "Martin Luther King Jr. and the 'I Have a Dream Speech,'," last viewed December 1, 2020, https://www.archives.gov/nyc/exhibit/mlk.
3. National Archives and Records Administration, "Statement from the President on the 50th Anniversary of the 16th Street Baptist Church Bombing in Birmingham, AL," last viewed December 1, 2020, https://obamawhitehouse.archives.gov/the-press-office/2013/09/15/statement-president-50th-anniversary-16th-street-baptist-church-bombing-.
4. National Archives and Records Administration, "The President John F. Kennedy Assassination Records Collection," last viewed December 1, 2020, https://www.archives.gov/research/jfk.
5. National Archives and Records Administration, "Record of the Week: Malcolm X Protests at DOJ," February 12, 2015, https://rediscovering-black-history.blogs.archives.gov/2015/02/12/rotw-malcolm-x-protests-doj/.
6. Jessie Kratz, "The National Archives and 1968: A Year of Triumph and Tragedy," National Archives and Records Administration, June 4, 2018, https://prologue.blogs.archives.gov/2018/06/04/the-national-archives-and-1968-a-year-of-triumph-and-tragedy/.
7. Pew Research Center, Social and Demographic Trends, "Parenting in America," December 17, 2015, http://www.pewsocialtrends.org/2015/12/17/1-the-american-family-today/.
8. FindLaw, "Obergefell v. Hodges, 14-556," June 26, 2015, https://caselaw.findlaw.com/summary/opinion/us-supreme court/2015/06/26/273882.html.
9. FindLaw, "Roe v. Wade Case Summary: What You Need to Know," last viewed December 18, 2020, https://supreme.findlaw.com/supreme-court-insights/roe-v--wade-case-summary--what-you-need-to-know.html.
10. Laurie D. Elam-Evans, PhD, Lilo T. Strauss, M.A., et al., "Abortion Surveillance - United States, 1999," Table 2, Centers for Disease Control and Prevention, November 29, 2002, last viewed November 16, 2020, https://www.cdc.gov/mmwr/preview/mmwrhtml/ss5109a1.htm.
11. Karen Pazol, PhD, Andreea A. Creanga, MD, PhD, et al., "Abortion Surveillance - United States, 2009," Table 1, Centers for Disease Control,"

November 23, 2012, last viewed November 16, 2020, https://www.cdc.gov/mmwr/preview/mmwrhtml/ss6108a1.htm?s_cid=ss6108a1_w.

12. Kortsmit K., Jatlaoui T.C., Mandel, M.G., et al., "Abortion Surveillance - United States, 2018," Table 1, Centers for Disease Control and Prevention, last viewed February 10, 2021, https://www.cdc.gov/mmwr/volumes/69/ss/ss6907a1.htm#contribAff.

13. Congressional Research Service, "American War and Military Operations Casualties: Lists and Statistics," Table I, Federation of American Scientists, July 29, 2020, https://fas.org/sgp/crs/natsec/RL32492.pdf.

14. The Advanced Law Enforcement Rapid Response Training (ALERRT) Center at Texas State University and the Federal Bureau of Investigation, U.S. Department of Justice, Washington, D.C., "Active Shooter Incidents in the United States in 2019," April 2020, https://www.fbi.gov/file-repository/active-shooter-incidents-in-the-us-2019 042820.pdf/view#:~:text=The%20FBI%20defines%20an%20active%20shooter%20as%20one,attempting%20to%20kill%20people%20in%20a%20populated%20area.

15. Federal Bureau of Investigation, "Quick Look: 277 Active Shooter Incidents in the United States from 2000 to 2018," last viewed November 10, 2020, https://www.fbi.gov/about/partnerships/office-of-partner-engagement/active-shooter-incidents-graphics.

16. Dave Lawler, Orion Rummler, "The Deadliest Mass Shootings in Modern U.S. History," Axios, April 27, 2020, https://www.axios.com/deadliest-mass-shootings-in-modern-us-history-3b2dfb67-7278-4082-a78c-d9fd-bef367f1.html.

17. Evita Duffy, "Capitol Hill Organized Protest: Vegan Utopia or Urban Anarchy," The Federalist, June 18, 2020, https://thefederalist.com/2020/06/18/capitol-hill-organized-protest-vegan-utopia-or-urban-anarchy/.

18. Department of Justice, "Opening Statement of Attorney General William P. Barr Before the House Judiciary Committee," July 28, 2020, https://www.justice.gov/opa/speech/opening-statement-attorney-general-william-p-barr-house-judiciary-committee.

19. Brian T. Moran, U.S. Attorney for the Western District of Washington, "Seattle Times Op-Ed Call to Defund Seattle Police are Alarming and Reckless," Department of Justice, July 27, 2020, https://www.justice.gov/opa/blog/calls-defund-seattle-police-are-alarming-and-reckless.

20 Abraham Lincoln Online, "The Perpetuation of Our Political Institutions: Address Before the Young Men's Lyceum of Springfield, Illinois January 27, 1838," last viewed August 6, 2020, http://www.abrahamlincolnonline.org/lincoln/speeches/lyceum.htm.
21 Centers for Disease Control and Prevention, "1918 Pandemic (H1N1 virus)," last viewed November 10, 2020, https://www.cdc.gov/flu/pandemic-resources/1918-pandemic-h1n1.html.
22 Centers for Disease Control and Prevention, "1957-1958 Pandemic (H2N2 virus)," last viewed November 10, 2020, https://www.cdc.gov/flu/pandemic-resources/1957-1958-pandemic.html.
23 Centers for Disease Control and Prevention, "1968 Pandemic (H3N2 virus)," last viewed November 10, 2020, https://www.cdc.gov/flu/pandemic-resources/1968-pandemic.html.
24 Centers for Disease Control and Prevention, "2009 H1N1 Pandemic (H1N1pdm09 virus)," last viewed November 10, 2020, https://www.cdc.gov/flu/pandemic-resources/2009-h1n1-pandemic.html.
25 Centers for Disease Control and Prevention, "The Global HIV / AIDS Pandemic, 2006," August 11, 2006, https://www.cdc.gov/mmwr/preview/mmwrhtml/mm5531a1.htm.
26 Centers for Disease Control and Prevention, "HIV Surveillance Report, 2016, volume 28," November 2017, http://www.cdc.gov/hiv/library/reports/hiv-surveillance.html, Table 2a & Table 17a.
27 Centers for Disease Control and Prevention, "Washington State Report First COVID-19 Death," February 29, 2020, https://www.cdc.gov/media/releases/2020/s0229-COVID-19-first-death.html
28 Centers for Disease Control and Prevention, "COVID Data Tracker," last viewed March 29, 2021, https://covid.cdc.gov/covid-data-tracker/#cases_totalcases.
29 World Health Organization, "WHO Coronavirus Disease (COVID-19) Dashboard," https://covid19.who.int, last viewed March 29, 2021.

Chapter 9—The Struggle Against Spiritual Forces
1 National Park Service, "We Have Met the Enemy and They Are Ours," May 24, 2016, https://www.nps.gov/articles/met-the-enemy-4.htm.
2 R. Albert Mohler Jr., *The Gathering Storm—Secularism, Culture, and the Church* (Nashville: Nelson Books, 2020), xvi.

3. Barna Group, "The End of Absolutes: America's New Moral Code," May 25, 2016, https://www.barna.com/research/the-end-of-absolutes-americas-new-moral-code/.

4. R. Albert Mohler Jr., *The Gathering Storm—Secularism, Culture, and the Church* (Nashville: Nelson Books, 2020), 22.

5. Glenn T. Stanton, "No, Christianity Doesn't Need to Endorse Homosexuality to Grow," The Federalist, May 6, 2019, https://thefederalist.com/2019/05/06/no-christianity-doesnt-need-endorse-homosexuality-grow/.

6. Alexander Griswold, "Adam Hamilton: Parts of Bible Don't Reflect God's Will," Juicy Ecumenism, April 25, 2014, https://juicyecumenism.com/2014/04/25/adam-hamilton-parts-of-bible-dont-reflect-gods-will/.

7. College Fix Staff, "11 Times Campus Speakers Were Shouted Down by Leftist Protesters This School Year," College Fix, April 24, 2018, https://www.thecollegefix.com/11-times-campus-speakers-were-shouted-down-by-leftist-protesters-this-school-year/.

8. Department of Justice, "Acting Assistant Attorney General John Gore Delivers Remarks at the Justice Department's Forum On Free Speech In Higher Education," September 17, 2018, https://www.justice.gov/opa/speech/acting-assistant-attorney-general-john-gore-delivers-remarks-justice-department-s-forum.

9. C-Span Video, "President Trump Delivers Remarks at Student Convention," June 23, 2020, https://www.c-span.org/video/?473331-1/president-trump-comments-protestors-taking-statues-repeats-nicknames-covid-19.

10. Michael Gryboski, "Franklin Graham: IRS Targeted Samaritan's Purse, Billy Graham Evangelistic Association," Christian Post, May 15, 2013, https://www.christianpost.com/news/franklin-graham-irs-targeted-samaritans-purse-billy-graham-evangelistic-association.html.

11. Jeff Schogol, "Army withdraws Franklin Graham Pentagon prayer day invitation," Stars and Stripes, April 22, 2010, https://www.stripes.com/news/army-withdraws-franklin-graham-pentagon-prayer-day-invitation-1.101569.

12. National Archives and Records Administration, "The Bill of Rights: A Transcription," last viewed December 28, 2020, https://www.archives.gov/founding-docs/bill-of-rights-transcript.

NOTES

13 FindLaw, "Engel V. Vitale (1962)," last viewed December 16, 2020, https://supreme.findlaw.com/supreme_court/landmark/engel.html.

14 U.S. Courts, "Similar Cases—Engel v. Vitale," last viewed November 28, 2020, https://www.uscourts.gov/educational-resources/educational-activities/similar-cases-engel-v-vitale.

15 Anthony J. Sebok, "The Controversy Over Alabama's Ten Commandments Statue, and the Nature of Justified Civil Disobedience," FindLaw, August 25, 2003, https://supreme.findlaw.com/legal-commentary/the-controversy-over-alabamas-ten-commandments-statue-and-the-nature-of-justified-civil-disobedience.html.

16 Editor, Christian News, "New Orleans City Council Officially Lifts Ban on Preaching After Sundown," August 4, 2013, https://christiannews.net/2013/08/04/new-orleans-city-council-officially-lifts-ban-on-preaching-after-sundown/.

17 Department of Justice, "Attorney General William P. Barr Delivers Remarks to the Law School and the de Nicola Center for Ethics and Culture at the University of Notre Dame," October 11, 2019, https://www.justice.gov/opa/speech/attorney-general-william-p-barr-delivers-remarks-law-school-and-de-nicola-center-ethics.

18 Luke Goodrich, *Free to Believe: The Battle over Religious Liberty in America* (Colorado Springs: Multnomah, 2019), 7.

19 Ibid., 59.

20 Christian Classics Ethereal Library, "Bible Reading by the Laity, Restrictions On," Calvin College, last updated May 10, 2004, https://ccel.org/s/schaff/encyc/encyc02/htm/iv.v.lxi.htm.

Chapter 10—Persecuting Messengers of the Truth

1 Grent C. Butler, PhD, General Editor, *Holman Bible Dictionary*, "Nero." (Nashville: Holman Bible Publishers 1991), 1018.

2 Ibid., 490.

3 C. F. Cruse, *Eusebius' Ecclesiastical History* (Peabody, MA: Hendrickson Publishers, 2000), 63.

4 Ibid., 60–61.

5 Editors, Christian History Magazine, "Christian History Timeline: Persecution in the Early Church," last viewed January 8, 2021, https://christianhistoryinstitute.org/magazine/article/persecution-in-early-church-timeline/.

NOTES

6   Christian Classics Ethereal Library, "Bible Reading by the Laity, Restrictions On," Calvin College, last updated May 10, 2004, https://ccel.org/s/schaff/encyc/encyc02/htm/iv.v.lxi.htm.

7   Greatsite.com, "John Wycliffe," last viewed January 21, 2021, https://www.greatsite.com/timeline-english-bible-history/john-wycliffe.html.

8   Greatsite.com, "William Tyndale," last viewed January 21, 2021, https://www.greatsite.com/timeline-english-bible-history/william-tyndale.html.

9   Samuel Smith, "1,202 Nigerian Christians Killed in First 6 Months of 2020: NGO Report," Christian Post, last viewed December 6, 2020, https://www.christianpost.com/news/1202-nigerian-christians-killed-in-first-6-months-of-2020-ngo-report.html.

10 Open Doors USA, "World Watchlist 2020," last viewed on November 3, 2020, https://www.opendoorsusa.org/wpcontent/uploads/2020/01/2020_World_Watch_List.pdf.

11 "Toleration in Old and New England, 3 June 1772," Founders Online, National Archives, last viewed January 16, 2021, https://founders.archives.gov/documents/Franklin/01-19-02-0114. [Original source: The Papers of Benjamin Franklin, vol. 19, January 1 through December 31, 1772, ed. William B. Willcox. New Haven and London: Yale University Press, New Haven and London, 1975, pp. 163–168.]

12 "82. A Bill for Establishing Religious Freedom, 18 June 1779," Founders Online, National Archives, last viewed January 16, 2021, https://founders.archives.gov/documents/Jefferson/01-02-02-0132-0004-0082. [Original source: The Papers of Thomas Jefferson, vol. 2, 1777–18 June 1779, ed. Julian P. Boyd. Princeton: Princeton University Press, 1950, pp. 545–553.]

13 National Park Service, Fort Matanzas National Monument, "The Massacre of the French," May 8, 2020, https://www.nps.gov/foma/learn/historyculture/the_massacre.htm.

14 National Archives and Records Administration, "Colonization and Settlement (1585-1763)," last viewed January 11, 2021, https://www.archives.gov/exhibits/american_originals/colony.html.

15 "Editorial Note," Founders Online, National Archives, last viewed January 16, 2021, https://founders.archives.gov/documents/Adams/05-02-02-0003-0002-0001. [Original source: The Adams Papers, Legal Papers of John Adams, vol. 2, Cases 31–62, ed. L. Kinvin Wroth and Hiller B. Zobel. Cambridge, MA: Harvard University Press, 1965, pp. 32–42.]

16 Samuel W. Rushay, Jr., "Harry Truman's History Lessons," National Archives and Records Administration, Spring 2009, https://www.archives.gov/publications/prologue/2009/spring/truman-history.html, 11.

17 "To Thomas Jefferson from Robert Semple, 24 October 1808," Founders Online, National Archives, last viewed January 16, 2021, https://founders.archives.gov/documents/Jefferson/99-01-02-8934. [This is an Early Access document from The Papers of Thomas Jefferson. It is not an authoritative final version.]

18 Missouri Secretary of State, Missouri State Archives, "The Missouri Mormon War," https://www.sos.mo.gov/archives/resources/mormon.asp, last viewed January 13, 2021.

19 Zachary M. Schrag, "Nativist Riots of 1844," Encyclopedia of Greater Philadelphia, last viewed January 18, 2021, https://philadelphiaencyclopedia.org/archive/nativist-riots-of-1844/.

20 U.S. Department of State, "1993 World Trade Center Bombing," February 21, 2019, https://www.state.gov/1993-world-trade-center-bombing/.

21 U.S. Government Accountability Office, "Countering Violent Extremism," April 6, 2017, https://www.gao.gov/assets/690/683984.pdf, 3.

22 Centers for Disease Control and Prevention, "Deaths in World Trade Center Terrorist Attacks—New York City, 2001," September 11, 2002, https://www.cdc.gov/mmwr/preview/mmwrhtml/mm51SPa6.htm.

Chapter 11—The State of the Union

1 Centers for Disease Control and Prevention, National Center for Health Statistics, "Table 44. Personal health care expenditures, by source of funds and type of expenditure: United States, selected years 1960–2017," last viewed October 27, 2020, https://www.cdc.gov/nchs/data/hus/2018/044.pdf, 4.

2 National Institute of Mental Health, "Major Depression," February 2019, https://www.nimh.nih.gov/health/statistics/major-depression.shtml, 2, 5.

3 Lisa J. Colpe, PhD, MPH, "Deaths of Despair: How Connecting Opioid Data Extends the Possibilities for Suicide Research," Centers for Disease Control and Prevention, April 2, 2020, https://www.cdc.gov/surveillance/blogs-stories/deaths-of-dispair.html.

4 National Institute of Mental Health, "Suicide," last viewed September 16, 2018, https://www.nimh.nih.gov/health/statistics/suicide.shtml.

5   Centers for Disease Control and Prevention, "Suicide Rising Across the US," last viewed September 16, 2018, https://www.cdc.gov/vitalsigns/suicide/index.html.
6   Centers for Disease Control and Prevention, "PMR Query System for Occupation (1999, 2003-2004, 2007-2014)," last viewed September 16, 2018, https://www.cdc.gov/niosh/topics/noms/query.html.
7   Centers for Disease Control and Prevention, "U.S. Drug Overdose Deaths Continue to Rise; Increase Fueled by Synthetic Opioids," March 29, 2018, https://www.cdc.gov/media/releases/2018/p0329-drug-overdose-deaths.html.
8   National Institute on Drug Abuse, "Overdose Death Rates," August 2018, https://www.drugabuse.gov/related-topics/trends-statistics/overdose-death-rates.
9   National Vital Statistics System, "Deaths and Mortality," Centers for Disease Control and Prevention, National Center for Health Statistics, last reviewed January 12, 2021, https://www.cdc.gov/nchs/fastats/deaths.htm.
10 Pew Forum, "In U.S., Decline of Christianity Continues at Rapid Pace - An update on America's Changing Religious Landscape," October 17, 2019, https://www.pewforum.org/2019/10/17/in-u-s-decline-of-christianity-continues-at-rapid-pace/.
11 Pew Research Center, "Global Christianity—A Report on the Size and Distribution of the World's Christian Population," December 19, 2011, https://www.pewforum.org/2011/12/19/global-christianity-exec/#:~:text=December%2019%2C%202011%20Global%20Christianity%20%E2%80%93%20A%20Report,the%20estimated%202010%20global%20population%20of%206.9%20billion.

Chapter 12—The Opportunity is Today
1   R. Albert Mohler Jr., *The Gathering Storm—Secularism, Culture, and the Church* (Nashville: Nelson Books, 2020), 21
2   Oswald Chambers, *My Utmost for His Highest* (Westwood, NJ: Barbour and Company, Inc, 1963), 77.
3   Ibid., 27.
4   Ibid., 243.
5   Ibid., 136.

6. David Kinnaman and Gabe Lyons, *UnChristian—What a New Generation Really Thinks About Christianity . . . and Why It Matters* (Grand Rapids, MI: Baker Books, 2007), 71.
7. Dr. Lynn Anderson, *They Smell Like Sheep—Spiritual Leadership for the 21st Century* (West Monroe, LA: Howard Publishing Co., 1997), 4.
8. Ibid., 24.
9. Judy A. Rumerman, "Human Space Flight: A Record of Achievement, 1961–1998," National Aeronautics and Space Administration, last viewed December 1, 2020, https://history.nasa.gov/SP-4225/documentation/hsf-record/hsf.htm, 4 & 23.
10. National Aeronautics and Space Administration, "Astronauts Launch from American Soil," last viewed December 5, 2020, https://earthobservatory.nasa.gov/images/146794/astronauts-launch-from-american-soil.
11. United States Courts, "Facts and Case Summary—Snyder v. Phelps," last viewed December 4, 2020, https://www.uscourts.gov/educational-resources/educational-activities/facts-and-case-summary-snyder-v-phelps.
12. Brandon Showalter, "Religion Contributes $1.2 Trillion to US Economy, More Than Top 10 Tech Companies Combined, Study Finds," Christian Post, September 16, 2016, https://www.christianpost.com/news/religion-contributes-trillion-us-economy-top-10-tech-companies-study-faith-counts-169649/.

Chapter 13—Retirement—A Golden Opportunity

1. Brian Jones, *Finding Favor—God's Blessings Beyond Health, Wealth, and Happiness* (Downers Grove, IL: InterVarsity Press, 2018), 12.
2. David Platt, *Radical—Taking Back Your Faith from the American Dream* (Colorado Springs, CO: Multnomah Books, 2010), 35-36.
3. Stu Weber, *Tender Warrior* (Sisters, OR: Multnomah Books, 1993), 22, 24.
4. Prison Fellowship Ministries, "Our Founder, Chuck Colson," last viewed January 12, 2021, https://www.prisonfellowship.org/about/chuck-colson/.

Chapter 14 - Your Assigned Area of Operation

1. National Archives and Records Administration, "The Bill of Rights: A Transcription," last viewed December 28, 2020, https://www.archives.gov/founding-docs/bill-of-rights-transcript.
2. Barna Group, "Five Years Later: 9/11 Attacks Show No Lasting Influence on Americans' Faith," August 28, 2006, https://www.barna.com/research/five-years-later-911-attacks-show-no-lasting-influence-on-americans-faith/.
3. Department of Justice, "Attorney General William P. Barr Delivers Remarks to the Law School and the de Nicola Center for Ethics and Culture at the University of Notre Dame," October 11, 2019, https://www.justice.gov/opa/speech/attorney-general-william-p-barr-delivers-remarks-law-school-and-de-nicola-center-ethics.
4. R. Albert Mohler Jr., *The Gathering Storm—Secularism, Culture, and the Church* (Nashville: Nelson Books, 2020), 91
5. Gary Inrig, *True North—Discovering God's Way in a Changing World* (Grand Rapids, MI: Discovery House Publishers, 2002), 20.
6. Ibid., 65.
7. Ibid., 49.
8. Francis Chan, *Crazy Love* (Colorado Springs, CO: David C. Cook, 2008), 19.

Conclusion

1. Oswald Chambers, *My Utmost for His Highest* (Westwood, NJ: Barbour and Company, Inc, 1963), 14.

www.ingramcontent.com/pod-product-compliance
Lightning Source LLC
Chambersburg PA
CBHW030037100526
44590CB00011B/236